THE FOLGER LIBRARY
SHAKESPEARE

Designed to make Shakespeare's classic plays available to the general reader, each edition contains a reliable text with modernized spelling and punctuation, scene-by-scene plot summaries, and explanatory notes clarifying obscure and obsolete expressions. An interpretive essay and accounts of Shakespeare's life and theater form an instructive preface to each play.

Louis B. Wright, General Editor, was the Director of the Folger Shakespeare Library from 1948 until his retirement in 1968. He is the author of *Middle-Class Culture in Elizabethan England, Religion and Empire, Shakespeare for Everyman,* and many other books and essays on the history and literature of the Tudor and Stuart periods.

Virginia Lamar, Assistant Editor, served as research assistant to the Director and Executive Secretary of the Folger Shakespeare Library from 1946 until her death in 1968. She is the author of *English Dress in the Age of Shakespeare* and *Travel and Roads in England,* and coeditor of William Strachey's *Historie of Travell into Virginia Britania.*

The Folger Shakespeare Library

The Folger Shakespeare Library in Washington, D.C., a research institute founded and endowed by Henry Clay Folger and administered by the Trustees of Amherst College, contains the world's largest collection of Shakespeareana. Although the Folger Library's primary purpose is to encourage advanced research in history and literature, it has continually exhibited a profound concern in stimulating a popular interest in the Elizabethan period.

GENERAL EDITOR

LOUIS B. WRIGHT

Director, Folger Shakespeare Library, 1948–1968

ASSISTANT EDITOR

VIRGINIA A. LaMAR

Executive Secretary, Folger Shakespeare Library, 1946–1968

The Folger Library General Reader's Shakespeare

THE TRAGEDY OF
OTHELLO
THE MOOR OF VENICE

by WILLIAM
SHAKESPEARE

WASHINGTON SQUARE PRESS
PUBLISHED BY POCKET BOOKS NEW YORK

A Washington Square Press Publication of
POCKET BOOKS, a Simon & Schuster division of
GULF & WESTERN CORPORATION
1230 Avenue of the Americas, New York, N.Y. 10020

ISBN: 0-671-44151-5

First Pocket Books printing September, 1957

35   34   33   32   31   30

WASHINGTON SQUARE PRESS, WSP and colophon are trademarks
of Simon & Schuster.

Printed in the U.S.A.

Preface

This edition of *Othello* is designed to make available a readable text of one of Shakespeare's greatest plays. In the centuries since Shakespeare many changes have occurred in the meanings of words, and some clarification of Shakespeare's vocabulary may be helpful. To provide the reader with necessary notes in the most accessible format, we have placed them on the pages facing the text that they explain. We have tried to make these notes as brief and simple as possible. Preliminary to the text we have also included a brief statement of essential information about Shakespeare and his stage. Readers desiring more detailed information should refer to the books suggested in the references, and if still further information is needed, the bibliographies in those books will provide the necessary clues to the literature of the subject.

L.B.W.
V.L.F.

December 17, 1956

THE SIGNIFICANCE OF
OTHELLO

SHAKESPEARE'S TRAGEDY *Othello* has enjoyed popularity on the stage from the author's time to our own. It has remained a living drama over the centuries because it treats emotions that are universal and persistent in human nature. Its characters do not exist on a plane far removed from ordinary life; we are not asked to witness the conflict of kings and conspirators beyond the experience of everyday people; we are not involved in the consequences of disasters on a cosmic scale; what we witness is a struggle between good and evil, the demonstration of love, tenderness, jealousy, and hate in terms that are humanly plausible. *Othello* is a drama of pathos and pity rather than a tragedy of character in which some tragic flaw brings about the doom of the hero. The latter concept was the Greek ideal of pure tragedy. *Othello* does not conform to this classic definition of tragedy, which had for its protagonist some noble hero of high birth, a king or a prince, in a contest with gods or supermen. Though Shakespeare follows tradition sufficiently to make both the hero and the heroine of his play personages of prominence, they are human rather than superhuman, and their reactions are the reactions understood by any spectator in the audience. The concentration upon elemental emotions presented in moving and poetic language has given *Othello* its great popularity, both as a play to be seen and a book to be read by men and women, for three and a half centuries.

Othello has been described as Shakespeare's most perfect play. Critics of dramatic structure have praised it for its attention to the main theme without irrelevant distractions. Many Elizabethan plays had rambling sub-plots and much extraneous detail to amuse the ground-lings. *Othello* avoids all irrelevancies and the action moves swiftly from the first scene to the denouement. We never get lost in a multiplicity of incidents or a multitude of characters. Our attention remains centered on the arch villainy of Iago and his plot to plant in Othello's mind a corroding belief in his wife's faithlessness. In the working out of this plot, the author maintains suspense until the very end. The characters are distinctly drawn and the contrasts are clear and vivid. No obscurity in language, characterization, or presentation befuddles the spectator or the reader. In *Othello*, Shakespeare displayed the skill of a genius in play construction, a skill that he himself did not always take the trouble to exert. It is no wonder that *Othello* is a favorite of playgoers and readers alike.

Elizabethan dramatists were fond of portraying characters of consummate evil, and if they could lay the scenes in Italy, all the better, because the literature and legend of the day were filled with stories of the wickedness of Italy. Garbled interpretations of Machiavelli were quoted in proof of cynical ruthlessness. The deeds of Alexander VI, Cesare Borgia, Lucrezia Borgia, and many others were a stock in trade of storytellers fascinated with sensational iniquity. To Englishmen, both those who traveled and those who stayed at home and listened, Renaissance Italy possessed a hypnotic

fascination. Venice especially had a glamor and an
interest beyond the normal. Every returning traveler
had a tall tale to tell about the beauty and com-
plaisance of Venetian women, the passion, jealousy, and
quick anger of Venetian men, and the bloody deeds of
Venetian bravoes. For Shakespeare to give his play an
initial setting in Venice was to gain immediate interest. Every Elizabethan spectator was ready to expect
some sensational revelation.

Iago at once captures the attention of the spectator.
He is the personification of the villain that Elizabethans
had come to expect from Italian short stories and from
Machiavellian commentary. Villains of this type, as
well as those of domestic origin, had long been popular
on the stage. From the days of the mystery and moral-
ity plays, the characters personifying evil invariably
had gripped the attention of audiences, for iniquity
always stirs more popular excitement than virtue. The
preacher who paints a vivid picture of wickedness has
a larger congregation than one who discourses on the
beauties of Paradise. Shakespeare had already achieved
success in the portrayal of villains, notably in the characterization of King Richard III, with whom one should
compare Iago because of his conscious preference for
evil ways to gain his desires. To give some shadow of
plausibility to Iago's wickedness, Shakespeare has him
declare his hatred of Othello for passing him over and
promoting Cassio, and he has Iago hint that Othello
may have been intimate with his wife, Emilia, but this
latter suggestion is almost an afterthought of Iago's to
rationalize a hate and envy that are part of his nature.
To make the irony deeper, Shakespeare gives Iago an
outward appearance of honest virtue and has Othello

call him "honest Iago." Othello himself is by nature courageous, open, generous, unsuspecting—and naïve. Desdemona is warmhearted, tender, faithful, and much in love with her husband. No thought is further from her mind than the infidelity that Iago suggests to Othello. The suspense of the play increases as we watch Iago subtly poison Othello's mind and witness Desdemona's bewilderment, despair, and ultimate death, and this suspense is retained until the last lines when the spectator is left to imagine the tortures awaiting Iago, who is dragged off the stage to judgment.

THE HISTORY OF THE PLAY

CONTROVERSIES have raged about the date of the first performance of *Othello*. John Payne Collier, the nineteenth-century scholar and forger, faked an entry in an old record to "prove" the performance of *Othello* before the Queen at Harefield on August 2, 1602. The antiquarian Peter Cunningham published a statement from an old manuscript, now lost, that *Othello* was performed at Court on November 1, 1604. Edmund Malone, one of the most trustworthy scholars of the eighteenth century, declared that he had "indisputable evidence" that the play was acted in 1604. The best modern opinion is that the first performance of the play was probably in 1604 and that it was composed between 1601 and the date of performance.

The play was immediately popular and records of its performance show that its popularity continued through the seventeenth century, except for the period when plays were outlawed during the Puritan regime. After the Restoration of Charles II, in 1660, and the reopening of the London theatres, women for the first time replaced the boy actors who had played female roles in Elizabethan times. The first woman seen on a public stage in London played Desdemona, and the part became a favorite with actresses from that time onward. Some of the most famous actresses starred as Desdemona. The first actor to take the part of Othello is supposed to have been Shakespeare's colleague Richard Burbage, and it was a favorite role of many actors after him. The American Negro actor Ira Aldridge between 1826 and 1852 made a reputation playing Othello in England and Germany. Nearly a century later Paul Robeson played Othello successfully in England and later in the United States.

The source of Shakespeare's play was a short story from the *Hecatommithi*, a collection of tales brought out in 1565 by an Italian named Giovanni Battista Giraldi, more often called Cinthio. Whether Shakespeare could read Italian nobody knows, but the *Hecatommithi* was widely known in England and was used by other dramatists. If he could not read it himself, he could learn the outline of the story from someone who could translate it. The story is from that section of the collection dealing with "The Unfaithfulness of Husbands and Wives," a fruitful place for an Elizabethan to look for a plot. In the original, the only character given a name is Disdemona, a wife described as very beautiful and virtuous. The origin of the name Othello is obscure. Iago of course is an Italian form of James. Shakespeare gave his characters names that he supposed to be typically Italian as befitted the setting of his play.

Much ink has been spilled in the debate over the

color of Othello and what physical characteristics Shakespeare attributed to a "Moor." Actors who have portrayed the part have also shown much concern over their make-up. There is little to indicate that Shakespeare or his contemporaries would have interpreted the union of Othello and Desdemona as a problem in mixed marriage or would have regarded the racial differences as of vital interest. To the Elizabethans, Othello was an exotic, and such interest as always attaches to exotics attached to him. On the Elizabethan stage, a Russian or a Pole would probably have been an even stranger character than a Moor.

The interest in Moors was persistent because of the stories of the Moors in Spain, and more recently because of the forays of Moorish pirates in the Mediterranean and even as far afield as the English Channel. Moorish soldiers had taken part in the siege of Malta by the Turks in 1565, a struggle which Beaumont and Fletcher dramatized in 1618 in a play called *The Knight of Malta*. Englishmen had also had their interest aroused in Morocco by the Battle of Alcazar in 1578, in which Dom Sebastian, the King of Portugal, lost his life, the climax of his ill-fated invasion of Morocco. George Peele wrote a play called *The Battle of Alcazar*, which was acted about 1589; and a number of other dramatic pieces concerned themselves with Moors or Moorish themes. Shakespeare took Othello's appellation, "the Moor," from the Italian tale that was his source.

To an Elizabethan, a Moor was a swarthy man. Shakespeare and his contemporaries were not anthropologists and they were not concerned with questions of "race." The debate as to whether Shakespeare in-

An Italian artist's conception of a noble Moor.
From Vecellio, *De gli habiti antichi* (1590).

tended Othello to be a Berber or a Negro is beside the point. Shakespeare neither knew nor cared. To him a Moor was a dark, exotic man, and he might call him "black," for he once declared that his brunette ladylove in Sonnet 147 was "as black as hell." In using this descriptive phrase Shakespeare was reacting against the convention of the period which attributed the height of beauty to fair skin and golden hair. Actors who chose to play Othello as a coal-black man, however, were probably taking Shakespeare's words too literally. Shakespeare was not trying in *Othello* to emphasize any racial differences between the hero and the heroine, though the differences in their backgrounds provide Iago with plausible suggestions for Desdemona's alleged disaffection. Othello, as Shakespeare characterizes him, is a soldier of fortune from a foreign country, a hero, who wins Desdemona by his bearing and the romantic recital of his adventures in strange lands. When enemies of Othello want to abuse him, they speak opprobriously of his alien looks and wonder that Desdemona could love so strange a man, but that is part of the reality of the characterization, not a hint on Shakespeare's part of "racism." The unhappy times when men would read some suggestion of racial prejudice into every piece of literature concerned with alien characters lay some centuries ahead.

Actors of the seventeenth and eighteenth centuries traditionally played Othello black, usually in some strange Oriental garb. In the later years of the eighteenth century, John Philip Kemble portrayed Othello as a dark-skinned Oriental type and dressed for the part in a mixture of British military uniform and Turkish trousers and turban. A few years later Edmund Kean began a tradition of playing Othello as a lighter-skinned Oriental in a costume that was vaguely "Moorish." Othello, of course, was in the military service of Venice and would be supposed to wear the military dress appropriate to a Venetian officer, but actors generally tried to suggest in some fashion the Oriental or Moorish background of the hero.

THE TEXT OF THE PLAY

Othello was first printed in 1622, one year before the First Folio, the collected edition of Shakespeare's plays, appeared. The 1622 quarto version was printed by Nicholas Oakes for Thomas Walkley and its title page declared that it had "been divers times acted at the Globe, and at the Blackfriars." The First Folio and the First Quarto texts are equally authoritative; both appear to derive from playhouse manuscripts. The Folio version contains about 160 lines omitted from the Quarto, but in many instances the Quarto provides better readings. Two later quartos (1630 and 1655) were probably based on the two earlier texts. In the preparation of the present edition, the editors in general have followed the Folio, but they have made corrections based on the First Quarto when its readings seemed preferable; they have modernized spelling and altered punctuation to give the sense that was intended.

Neither the Folio nor the Quarto text contains settings for the various scenes, and stage directions are few and inadequate. Accordingly, settings and stage directions have been added to illuminate the action. These and additions to directions adopted from the original texts are enclosed in square brackets.

The numbering of lines is literally line by line and therefore does not agree with the lineation in most concordances, which follow the convention of counting two consecutive half-lines of verse as one metrical line.

THE AUTHOR

WHEN William Shakespeare's *Othello* was performed in 1604, the author was already one of the most popular dramatists of his day, as well as an actor and a producer. Most of his best comedies, his great history plays, and some of his finest tragedies were behind him. Only *King Lear, Macbeth, Antony and Cleopatra, Coriolanus, Timon of Athens, Pericles, Cymbeline, The Winter's Tale, The Tempest,* and *Henry VIII* were yet to be written.

Shakespeare was so well known as a literary and dramatic craftsman that Francis Meres, a young preacher, in a volume called *Palladis Tamia: Wits Treasury* (1598), referred in flattering terms to him as "mellifluous and honey-tongued Shakespeare," famous for his *Venus and Adonis,* his *Lucrece,* and "his sugared sonnets," which were circulating "among his private friends." Meres observes further that "as Plautus and Seneca are accounted the best for comedy and tragedy among the Latins, so Shakespeare among the English is the most excellent in both kinds for the stage," and he mentions a dozen plays that had made a name for Shakespeare. He concludes with the remark "that the Muses would speak with Shakespeare's fine filed phrase if they would speak English."

To those acquainted with the history of the Elizabethan and Jacobean periods, it is incredible that any-

THE
Tragœdy of Othello,
The Moore of Venice.

As it hath beene diuerse times acted at the
Globe, and at the Black-Friers, by
his Maiesties Seruants.

Written by VVilliam Shakespeare.

LONDON,
Printed by *N. O.* for *Thomas Walkley*, and are to be sold at his
shop, at the Eagle and Child, in Brittans Bursse.
1622.

The title page of the First Quarto of *Othello* (1622).

one should be so naïve or ignorant as to doubt the reality of Shakespeare as the author of the plays that bear his name. Yet so much nonsense has been written about other "candidates" for the plays that it is well to remind readers that no credible evidence that would stand up in a court of law has ever been adduced to prove either that Shakespeare did not write his plays or that anyone else wrote them. All the theories offered for the authorship of Francis Bacon, the Earl of Derby, the Earl of Oxford, the Earl of Hertford, Christopher Marlowe, and a score of other candidates are mere conjectures spun from the active imaginations of persons who confuse hypothesis and conjecture with evidence.

As Meres' statement of 1598 indicates, Shakespeare was already a popular playwright whose name carried weight at the box office. The obvious reputation of Shakespeare as early as 1598 makes the effort to prove him a myth one of the most absurd in the history of human perversity.

The anti-Shakespeareans talk darkly about a plot of vested interests to maintain the authorship of Shakespeare. Nobody has any vested interest in Shakespeare, but every scholar is interested in the truth and in the quality of evidence advanced by special pleaders who set forth hypotheses in place of facts.

The anti-Shakespeareans base their arguments upon a few simple premises, all of them false. These false premises are that Shakespeare was an unlettered yokel without any schooling, that nothing is known about Shakespeare, and that only a noble lord or the equivalent in background could have written the plays. The facts are that more is known about Shakespeare than about most dramatists of his day, that he had a very good education acquired in the Stratford Grammar School, that the plays show no evidence of profound book learning, and that the knowledge of kings and courts evident in the plays is no greater than any intelligent young man could have picked up at second hand. Most anti-Shakespeareans are naïve and betray an obvious snobbery. The author of their favorite plays, they imply, must have had a college diploma framed and hung on his study wall like the one in their dentist's office, and obviously so great a writer must have had a title or some equally significant evidence of exalted social background. They forget that genius has a way of cropping up in unexpected places and that none of the great creative writers of the world got his inspiration in a college or university course.

William Shakespeare was the son of John Shakespeare of Stratford-upon-Avon, a substantial citizen of that small but busy market town in the center of the rich agricultural county of Warwick. John Shakespeare kept a shop, what we would call a general store; he dealt in wool and other produce and gradually acquired property. As a youth, John Shakespeare had learned the trade of glover and leather worker. There is no contemporary evidence that the elder Shakespeare was a butcher, though the anti-Shakespeareans like to talk about the ignorant "butcher's boy of Stratford." Their only evidence is a statement by gossipy John Aubrey, more than a century after William Shakespeare's birth, that young William followed his father's trade and when he killed a calf "he would do it in a high style and make a speech." We would like to believe the story true, but Aubrey is not a very credible witness.

John Shakespeare probably continued to operate a

farm at Snitterfield that his father had leased. He married Mary Arden, daughter of his father's landlord, a man of some property. The third of their eight children was William, baptized on April 26, 1564, and probably born three days before. At least it is conventional to celebrate April 23 as his birthday.

The Stratford records give considerable information about John Shakespeare. We know that he held several municipal offices including those of alderman and mayor. In 1580 he was in some sort of legal difficulty and was fined for neglecting a summons of the Court of Queen's Bench requiring him to appear at Westminster and be bound over to keep the peace.

As a citizen and alderman of Stratford, John Shakespeare was entitled to send his son to the grammar school free. Though the records are lost, there can be no reason to doubt that this is where young William received his education. As any student of the period knows, the grammar schools provided the basic education in Latin learning and literature. The Elizabethan grammar school is not to be confused with modern grammar schools. Many cultivated men of the day received all their formal education in the grammar schools. At the universities in this period a student would have received little training that would have inspired him to be a creative writer. At Stratford young Shakespeare would have acquired a familiarity with Latin and some little knowledge of Greek. He would have read Latin authors and become acquainted with the plays of Plautus and Terence. Undoubtedly in this period of his life he received that stimulation to read and explore for himself the world of ancient and modern history which he later utilized in his plays. The

youngster who does not acquire this type of intellectual
curiosity *before* college days rarely develops the kind
of mind Shakespeare demonstrated as a result of a
college course. His learning in books was anything but
profound, but he clearly had the probing curiosity that
sent him in search of information, and he had a keen-
ness in the observation of nature and of humankind that
finds reflection in his poetry.

There is little documentation for Shakespeare's boy-
hood. There is little reason why there should be. Nobody knew that he was going to be a dramatist about
whom any scrap of information would be prized in the
centuries to come. He was merely an active and vigor-
ous youth of Stratford, perhaps assisting his father in
his business, and no Boswell bothered to write down
facts about him. The most important record that we
have is a marriage license issued by the Bishop of
Worcester on November 28, 1582, to permit William
Shakespeare to marry Anne Hathaway, seven or eight
years his senior; furthermore, the Bishop permitted the
marriage after reading the banns only once, instead of
three times—evidence of the desire for haste. The
need was explained on May 26, 1583, when the
christening of Susanna, daughter of William and Anne
Shakespeare, was recorded at Stratford. Two years
later, on February 2, 1585, the records show the birth
of twins to the Shakespeares, a boy and a girl who
were christened Hamnet and Judith.

What William Shakespeare was doing in Stratford
during the early years of his married life, or when
he went to London, we do not know. It has been con-
jectured that he tried his hand at schoolteaching, but
that is a mere guess. There is a legend that he left

Stratford to escape a charge of poaching in the park of
Sir Thomas Lucy at Charlecote, though there is no
proof of this. There is also a legend that when first
he came to London, he earned his living by holding
horses outside a playhouse and presently was given
employment inside, but there is nothing better than
eighteenth-century hearsay for this. How Shakespeare
broke into the London theatres as dramatist and actor
we do not know. But lack of information is not surpris-
ing, for Elizabethans did not write their autobiogra-
phies, and we know even less about the lives of many
writers and some men of affairs than we know about
Shakespeare. By 1592 he was so well established and
popular that he incurred the envy of the dramatist and
pamphleteer Robert Greene, who referred to him as
an "upstart crow . . . in his own conceit the only
Shakescene in a country." From this time onward
contemporary allusions and references in legal docu-
ments enable the scholar to chart Shakespeare's career
with greater accuracy than is possible with most other
Elizabethan dramatists.

By 1594 Shakespeare was a member of the company
of actors known then as the Lord Chamberlain's Men.
After the accession of James I, in 1603, the company
would have the sovereign for their patron and would
be known as the King's Men. During the period of
its greatest prosperity this company would have as its
principal theatres the Globe and the Blackfriars.
Shakespeare was both an actor and a shareholder in the
company. He thus had three sources of income: from
the sale of his plays to the company, from his wages as
an actor, and from his share of the profits of the
theatrical company. Tradition has assigned him such

acting roles as Adam in *As You Like It* and the Ghost in *Hamlet*, a modest place on the stage that suggests he may have had other duties in the management of the company. Such conclusions, however, are based on surmise.

What we do know is that his plays were popular and that he was highly successful in his triple vocation. His first play may have been *The Comedy of Errors,* acted perhaps in 1591. Certainly this was one of his earliest plays. The three parts of *Henry VI* were acted sometime between 1590 and 1592. Critics are not in agreement about precisely how much Shakespeare wrote of these three plays. *Richard III* probably dates from 1593. With this play Shakespeare captured the imagination of Elizabethan audiences, then enormously interested in historical plays. With *Richard III,* Shakespeare also gave an interpretation pleasing to the Tudors of the rise to power of the grandfather of Queen Elizabeth. From this time onward, Shakespeare's plays followed on the stage in rapid succession: *Titus Andronicus, The Taming of the Shrew, The Two Gentlemen of Verona, Love's Labour's Lost, Romeo and Juliet, Richard II, A Midsummer Night's Dream, King John, The Merchant of Venice, Henry IV* (Pts. I and II), *Much Ado About Nothing, Henry V, Julius Caesar, As You Like It, Twelfth Night, Hamlet, The Merry Wives of Windsor, All's Well That Ends Well, Measure for Measure, Othello, King Lear,* and nine others that followed before Shakespeare retired completely, about 1613.

In the course of his career in London, he made enough money to enable him to return to Stratford with a competence. His purchase on May 4, 1597, of New

Place, then the next to largest dwelling in Stratford, a "pretty house of brick and timber," with a handsome garden, indicates his increasing prosperity. There his wife and children lived while he busied himself in the London theatres. The summer before he acquired New Place his life was darkened by the death of his only son, Hamnet, a child of eleven. In May, 1602, Shakespeare purchased one hundred and seven acres of fertile farmland near Stratford and a few months later bought a cottage and garden across the alley from New Place. About 1611, he seems to have returned permanently to Stratford, for the next year a legal document refers to him as "William Shakespeare of Stratford-upon-Avon . . . gentleman." To achieve the desired appellation of gentleman, William Shakespeare had seen to it that the College of Heralds in 1596 granted his father a coat of arms. In one step he thus became a second-generation gentleman.

Shakespeare's daughter Susanna made a good match in 1607 with Dr. John Hall, a prominent and prosperous Stratford physician. His second daughter, Judith, did not marry until she was thirty-two years old, and then, under somewhat scandalous circumstances, she married Thomas Quiney, a Stratford vintner. On March 25, 1616, Shakespeare made his will, bequeathing his landed property to Susanna, £300 to Judith, certain sums to other relatives, and his second-best bed to his wife, Anne. Much has been made of the second-best bed, but the legacy probably indicates only that Anne liked that particular bed. Shakespeare, following the practice of the time, may have already arranged with Susanna for his wife's care. Finally, on April 23, 1616, the anniversary of his birth, William Shakespeare died, and he was buried on April 25 within the chancel of Trinity Church, as befitted an honored citizen. On August 6, 1623, a few months before the publication of the collected edition of Shakespeare's plays, Anne Shakespeare joined her husband in death.

THE PUBLICATION OF HIS PLAYS

DURING his lifetime Shakespeare made no effort to publish any of his plays, though eighteen appeared in print in single-play editions known as quartos. Some of these are corrupt versions known as "bad quartos." No quarto, so far as is known, had the author's approval. Plays were not considered "literature" any more than radio and television scripts today are considered literature. Dramatists sold their plays outright to the theatrical companies and it was usually considered in the company's interest to keep plays from getting into print. To achieve a reputation as a man of letters Shakespeare wrote his *Sonnets* and his narrative poems, *Venus and Adonis* and *The Rape of Lucrece,* but he probably never dreamed that his plays would establish his reputation as a literary genius. Only Ben Jonson, a man known for his colossal conceit, had the crust to call his plays *Works,* as he did when he published an edition in 1616. But men laughed at Ben Jonson.

After Shakespeare's death, two of his old colleagues in the King's Men, John Heming and Henry Condell, decided that it would be a good thing to print, in more accurate versions than were then available, the plays already published and eighteen additional plays not previously published in quarto. In 1623 appeared *Mr. William Shakespeares Comedies, Histories,*

& *Tragedies. Published according to the True Originall Copies. London. Printed by Isaac Iaggard and Ed. Blount.* This was the famous First Folio, a work that had the authority of Shakespeare's associates. The only play commonly attributed to Shakespeare that was omitted in the First Folio was *Pericles.* In their preface "To the great Variety of Readers," Heming and Condell state that whereas "you were abused with diverse stolen and surreptitious copies, maimed and deformed by the frauds and stealths of injurious impostors that exposed them, even those are now offered to your view cured and perfect of their limbs; and all the rest, absolute in their numbers, as he conceived them." What they used for printer's copy is one of the vexed problems of scholarship, and skilled bibliographers have devoted years of study to the question of the relation of the "copy" for the First Folio to Shakespeare's manuscripts. In some cases it is clear that the editors corrected printed quarto versions of the plays, probably by comparison with playhouse scripts. Whether these scripts were in Shakespeare's autograph is anybody's guess. No manuscript of any play in Shakespeare's handwriting has survived. Indeed, very few play manuscripts from this period by any author are extant. The Tudor and Stuart periods had not yet learned to prize autographs and authors' original manuscripts.

Since the First Folio contains eighteen plays not previously printed, it is the only source for these. For the other eighteen, which had appeared in quarto versions, the First Folio also has the authority of an edition prepared and overseen by Shakespeare's colleagues and professional associates. But since editorial standards in 1623 were far from strict, and Heming and Condell were actors rather than editors by profession, the texts are sometimes careless. The printing and proofreading of the First Folio also left much to be desired, and some garbled passages have to be corrected and emended. The "good" quarto texts have to be taken into account in preparing a modern edition.

Because of the great popularity of Shakespeare through the centuries the First Folio has become a prized book, but it is not a very rare one, for it is estimated that 238 copies are extant. The Folger Shakespeare Library, in Washington, D.C., has seventy-nine copies of the First Folio, collected by the founder, Henry Clay Folger, who believed that a collation of as many texts as possible would reveal significant facts about the text of Shakespeare's plays. Dr. Charlton Hinman, using an ingenious machine of his own invention for mechanical collating, has made many discoveries that throw light on Shakespeare's text and on printing practices of the day.

The probability is that the First Folio of 1623 had an edition of between 1,000 and 1,250 copies. It is believed that it sold for £1, which made it an expensive book, for £1 in 1623 was equivalent to something between $40 and $50 in modern purchasing power.

During the seventeenth century, Shakespeare was sufficiently popular to warrant three later editions in folio size, the Second Folio of 1632, the Third Folio of 1663-1664, and the Fourth Folio of 1685. The Third Folio added six other plays ascribed to Shakespeare, but these are apocryphal.

THE THEATRES in which Shakespeare's plays were performed were vastly different from those we know today. The stage was a platform that jutted out into the area now occupied by the first rows of seats on the main floor, what is called the "orchestra" in America and the "pit" in England. This platform had no curtain to come down at the ends of acts and scenes. And although simple stage properties were available, the Elizabethan theatre lacked both the machinery and the elaborate movable scenery of the modern theatre. In the rear of the platform stage was a curtained area that could be used as an inner room, a tomb, or any such scene that might be required. A balcony above this inner room, and perhaps balconies on the sides of the stage, could represent the upper deck of a ship, the entry to Juliet's room, or a prison window. A trap door in the stage provided an entrance for ghosts and devils from the nether regions, and a similar trap in the canopied structure over the stage, known as the "heavens," made it possible to let down angels on a rope. These primitive stage arrangements help to account for many elements in Elizabethan plays. For example, since there was no curtain, the dramatist frequently felt the necessity of writing into his play action to clear the stage at the ends of acts and scenes. The funeral march at the end of *Hamlet* is not there merely for atmosphere; Shakespeare had to get the corpses off the stage. The lack of scenery also freed the dramatist from undue concern about the exact location of his sets, and the physical relation of his various settings to each other did not have to be worked out with the same precision as in the modern theatre.

Before London had buildings designed exclusively for theatrical entertainment, plays were given in inns and taverns. The characteristic inn of the period had an inner courtyard with rooms opening onto balconies overlooking the yard. Players could set up their temporary stages at one end of the yard and audiences could find seats on the balconies out of the weather. The poorer sort could stand or sit on the cobblestones in the yard, which was open to the sky. The first theatres followed this construction, and throughout the Elizabethan period the large public theatres had a yard in front of the stage open to the weather, with two or three tiers of covered balconies extending around the theatre. This physical structure again influenced the writing of plays. Because a dramatist wanted the actors to be heard, he frequently wrote into his play orations that could be delivered with declamatory effect. He also provided spectacle, buffoonery, and broad jests to keep the riotous groundlings in the yard entertained and quiet.

In another respect the Elizabethan theatre differed greatly from ours. It had no actresses. All women's roles were taken by boys, sometimes recruited from the boys' choirs of the London churches. Some of these youths acted their roles with great skill and the Elizabethans did not seem to be aware of any incongruity. The first actresses on the professional English stage appeared after the Restoration of Charles II, in 1660, when exiled Englishmen brought back from France practices of the French stage.

London in the Elizabethan period, as now, was the center of theatrical interest, though wandering actors from time to time traveled through the country performing in inns, halls, and the houses of the nobility. The first professional playhouse, called simply The Theatre, was erected by James Burbage, father of Shakespeare's colleague Richard Burbage, in 1576 on lands of the old Holywell Priory adjacent to Finsbury Fields, a playground and park area just north of the city walls. It had the advantage of being outside the city's jurisdiction and yet was near enough to be easily accessible. Soon after The Theatre was opened, another playhouse called The Curtain was erected in the same neighborhood. Both of these playhouses had open courtyards and were probably polygonal in shape.

About the time The Curtain opened, Richard Farrant, Master of the Chapel Royal at Windsor and of St. Paul's, conceived the idea of opening a "private" theatre in the old monastery buildings of the Blackfriars, not far from St. Paul's Cathedral in the heart of the city. This theatre was ostensibly to train the choir boys in plays for presentation at Court. Actually, Farrant managed to present plays to paying audiences and achieved considerable success until aristocratic neighbors complained and had the theatre closed. This first Blackfriars Theatre was significant, however, because it popularized the boy actors in a professional way and it paved the way for a second theatre in the Blackfriars, which Shakespeare's company took over more than thirty years later. By the last years of the sixteenth century, London had at least six professional theatres and still others were erected during the reign of James I.

The Globe Theatre, the playhouse that most people connect with Shakespeare, was erected early in 1599 on the Bankside, the area across the Thames from the

The Globe Playhouse.
From Visscher's *View of London* (1616).

city. Its construction had a dramatic beginning, for on the night of December 28, 1598, James Burbage's sons, Cuthbert and Richard, gathered together a crew who tore down the old theatre in Holywell and carted the timbers across the river to a site that they had chosen for a new playhouse. The reason for this clandestine operation was a row with the landowner over the lease to the Holywell property. The site chosen for the Globe was another playground outside of the city's jurisdiction, a region of somewhat unsavory character. Not far away was the Bear Garden, an amphitheatre devoted to the baiting of bears and bulls. This was also the region occupied by many houses of ill fame licensed by the Bishop of Winchester and the source of substantial revenue to him. But it was easily accessible either from London Bridge or by means of the cheap boats operated by the London watermen, and it had the great advantage of being beyond the authority of the Puritanical aldermen of London, who frowned on plays because they lured apprentices from work, filled their heads with improper ideas, and generally exerted a bad influence. The aldermen also complained that the crowds drawn together in the theatre helped to spread the plague.

The Globe was the handsomest theatre up to its time. It was a large octagonal building, like its predecessors open to the sky in the center, but capable of seating a large audience in its covered balconies. To erect and operate the Globe, the Burbages organized a syndicate composed of the leading members of the dramatic company, of which Shakespeare was a member. Since it was open to the weather and depended on natural light, plays had to be given in the afternoon. This caused no hardship in the long afternoons of an

English summer, but in the winter, the weather was a great handicap and discouraged all except the hardiest. For that reason, in 1608, Shakespeare's company was glad to take over the lease of the second Blackfriars Theatre, a substantial, roomy hall reconstructed within the framework of the old monastery building. This theatre was protected from the weather and its stage was artificially lighted by chandeliers of candles. This became the winter playhouse for Shakespeare's company and at once proved so popular that the congestion of traffic created an embarrassing problem. Stringent regulations had to be made for the movement of coaches in the vicinity. Shakespeare's company continued to use the Globe during the summer months. In 1613 a squib fired from a cannon during a performance of *Henry VIII* fell on the thatched roof and the Globe burned to the ground. The next year it was rebuilt.

London had other famous theatres. The Rose, just west of the Globe, was built by Philip Henslowe, a semi-literate denizen of the Bankside, who became one of the most important theatrical owners and producers of the Tudor and Stuart periods. What is more important for historians, he kept a detailed account book, which provides much of our information about theatrical history in his time. Another famous theatre on the Bankside was the Swan, which a Dutch priest, Johannes de Witt, visited in 1596. The crude drawing of the stage which he made was copied by his friend Arend van Buchell; it is one of the important pieces of contemporary evidence for theatrical construction. De Witt described the Swan as capable of holding three thousand spectators. Among the other theatres, the Fortune, north of the city, on Golding Lane, and the

Red Bull, even farther away from the city, off St. John's Street, were the most popular. The Red Bull, much frequented by apprentices, favored sensational and sometimes rowdy plays.

The actors who kept all of these theatres going were organized into companies under the protection of some noble patron. Traditionally actors had enjoyed a low reputation. In some of the ordinances they were classed as vagrants; in the phraseology of the time, "rogues, vagabonds, sturdy beggars, and common players" were all listed together as undesirables. To escape penalties often meted out to these characters, organized groups of actors managed to gain the protection of various personages of high degree. In the later years of Elizabeth's reign, a group flourished under the name of the Queen's Men; another group had the protection of the Lord Admiral and were known as the Lord Admiral's Men. Edward Alleyn, son-in-law of Philip Henslowe, was the leading spirit in the Lord Admiral's Men. Besides the adult companies, troupes of boy actors from time to time also enjoyed considerable popularity. Among these were the Children of Paul's and the Children of the Chapel Royal.

The company with which Shakespeare had a long association had for its patron Henry Carey, Lord Hunsdon, the Lord Chamberlain, and hence they were known as the Lord Chamberlain's Men. After the accession of James I, they became the King's Men. This company was the great rival of the Admiral's Men, managed by Henslowe and Alleyn.

All was not easy for the players in Shakespeare's time, for the aldermen of London were always eager for an excuse to close up the Blackfriars and any other

theatres in their jurisdiction. The theatres outside the
jurisdiction of London were not immune from inter-
ference, for they might be shut up by order of the
Privy Council for meddling in politics or for various
other offenses, or they might be closed in time of
plague lest they spread infection. During plague times
the actors usually went on tour and played the provinces
wherever they could find an audience. Particularly
frightening were the plagues of 1592-1594 and 1613,
when the theatres closed and the players, like many
other Londoners, had to take to the country.

Though players had a low social status, they enjoyed
great popularity and one of the favorite forms of entertainment at Court was the performance of plays.
To be commanded to perform at Court conferred great
prestige upon a company of players, and when plays
were published that fact was frequently noted. Many
of Shakespeare's plays were performed before the
sovereign and Shakespeare himself undoubtedly acted
in some of these plays.

REFERENCES FOR FURTHER READING

MANY READERS will want suggestions for further reading about Shakespeare and his times. The literature in
this field is enormous but a few references will serve as
guides to further study. A simple and useful little
book is Gerald Sanders, *A Shakespeare Primer* (New
York, 1950). More detailed but still not too voluminous
to be confusing is Hazelton Spencer, *The Art and Life
of William Shakespeare* (New York, 1940), which, like
Sanders' handbook, contains a brief annotated list of
useful books on various aspects of the subject. The
most detailed and scholarly work providing complete

factual information about Shakespeare is Sir Edmund Chambers, *William Shakespeare: A Study of Facts and Problems* (2 vols., Oxford, 1930). For detailed, factual information about the Elizabethan and seventeenth-century stages, the definitive reference works are Sir Edmund Chambers, *The Elizabethan Stage* (4 vols., Oxford, 1923) and Gerald E. Bentley, *The Jacobean and Caroline Stage* (5 vols., Oxford, 1941-56).

Although specialists disagree about details of stage construction, the reader will find essential information in John C. Adams, *The Globe Playhouse: Its Design and Equipment* (Barnes & Noble, 1961). A model of the Globe playhouse made by Dr. Adams is on permanent exhibition in the Folger Shakespeare Library, in Washington, D.C. The architecture of the Globe is treated in Irwin Smith, *Shakespeare's Globe Playhouse: A Modern Reconstruction in Text and Scale Drawings Based upon the Reconstruction of the Globe by John Cranford Adams* (New York, 1956). An easily read history of the early theatres is J. Q. Adams, *Shakespearean Playhouses: A History of English Theatres from the Beginnings to the Restoration* (Boston, 1917).

The following histories of the theatre will provide information about Shakespeare's plays in later periods: Alfred Harbage, *Theatre for Shakespeare* (Toronto, 1955); Esther Cloudman Dunn, *Shakespeare in America* (New York, 1939); George C. D. Odell, *Shakespeare from Betterton to Irving* (2 vols., London, 1921); Arthur Colby Sprague, *Shakespeare and the Actors: The Stage Business in His Plays (1660-1905)* (Cambridge, Mass., 1945); Leslie Hotson, *The Commonwealth and Restoration Stage* (Cambridge, Mass., 1928); Alwin Thaler, *Shakspere to Sheridan: A Book About the*

Theatre of Yesterday and To-day (Cambridge, Mass., 1922); Ernest Bradlee Watson, *Sheridan to Robertson: A Study of the 19th-Century London Stage* (Cambridge, Mass., 1926).

Harley Granville-Barker, *Prefaces to Shakespeare* (5 vols., London, 1927-48) provides stimulating critical discussion of the plays. An older classic of criticism is Andrew C. Bradley, *Shakespearean Tragedy: Lectures on Hamlet, Othello, King Lear, Macbeth* (London, 1904), which is now available in an inexpensive reprint (New York, 1955). Thomas M. Parrott, *Shakespearean Comedy* (New York, 1949) is scholarly and readable. Shakespeare's dramatizations of English history are examined in E. M. W. Tillyard, *Shakespeare's History Plays* (London, 1948). Lily Bess Campbell, *Shakespeare's "Histories," Mirrors of Elizabethan Policy* (San Marino, Calif., 1947) contains a more technical discussion of the same subject.

Interesting pictures as well as information about Shakespeare will be found in F. E. Halliday, *Shakespeare, a Pictorial Biography* (London, 1956).

A brief, clear, and accurate account of Tudor history is S. T. Bindoff, *The Tudors* in the Penguin series. A readable general history is G. M. Trevelyan, *The History of England,* first published in 1926 and available in many editions since. Trevelyan's *English Social History,* first published in 1942 and also available in many editions, provides fascinating information about England in all periods. Sir John Neale, *Queen Elizabeth* (London, 1934) is the best study of the great Queen. Various aspects of literature and society are treated in Louis B. Wright, *Middle-Class Culture in Elizabethan England* (Chapel Hill, N.C., 1935).

Dramatis Personae.

Duke of Venice.
Brabantio, [a Senator], father to Desdemona.
Senators.
Gratiano, [brother to Brabantio], } two noble
Lodovico, [kinsman to Brabantio], } Venetians.
Othello, the Moor.
Cassio, [his] honorable Lieutenant.
Iago, [Othello's Ancient], a villain.
Roderigo, a gulled gentleman.
Montano, [retiring] Governor of Cyprus.
Clown, [servant to Othello].

Desdemona, [daughter to Brabantio and], wife
    to Othello.
Emilia, wife to Iago.
Bianca, a courtesan.

Sailor, [Messenger, Herald, Officers, Gentle-
    men, Musicians, Attendants].

[SCENE: Venice; Cyprus.]

THE TRAGEDY OF

OTHELLO,

THE MOOR OF VENICE

ACT I

I. i. Iago reveals his hatred of Othello, caused in part by resentment because Cassio was preferred for the post of Othello's lieutenant while he was given the lesser post of ancient. He induces Roderigo, a disappointed suitor of Desdemona, daughter of the Venetian senator Brabantio, to inform Brabantio of his daughter's elopement with Othello, the Moor, who commands the Venetian forces about to embark for Cyprus to repel the Turks.

iiiiiiiiiiiiiiiiiiiiiiiiiiiiiiiiiiii

4. 'Sblood: God's blood

11. Off-capped to him: that is, pleaded Iago's case with hats in hand, as though they were Othello's inferiors

14. bombast circumstance: high-sounding but irrelevant rhetoric. An obsolete meaning for bombast is "cotton stuffing."

17. Nonsuits: denies the suit of; Certes: certainly

18. chose: chosen, an alternate form of the past participle, often used by Elizabethans.

ACT I

<hr />

Scene I. [Venice. A street.]

Enter *Roderigo* and *Iago*.

Rod. Tush, never tell me! I take it much unkindly
That thou, Iago, who hast had my purse
As if the strings were thine, shouldst know of this.
    Iago. 'Sblood, but you'll not hear me!
If ever I did dream of such a matter,   5
Abhor me.
    Rod. Thou told'st me thou didst hold him in thy hate.
    Iago. Despise me if I do not. Three great ones of the
        city,
In personal suit to make me his lieutenant,   10
Off-capped to him; and, by the faith of man,
I know my price, I am worth no worse a place.
But he, as loving his own pride and purposes,
Evades them with a bombast circumstance,
Horribly stuffed with epithets of war;   15
And, in conclusion,
Nonsuits my mediators; for, "Certes," says he,
"I have already chose my officer."
And what was he?

I

20. **arithmetician**: a student of tactics as revealed in military books, which were filled with arithmetical tables of organization.

22. **almost damned in a fair wife**: it is uncertain whether Shakespeare originally intended for Cassio to be married and forgot to delete this passage when he developed his plot otherwise, or whether this is a reference to Bianca's unsuccessful matrimonial pursuit of him. "Damned in a fair wife" reflects a proverbial attitude that a handsome wife was a source of trouble for her husband.

25-7. **unless the bookish theoric,/ Wherein the toged consuls can propose/ As masterly**: except in book theory, in which the statesmen of Venice are as adept. The toga (robe of state) symbolized peace.

28. **had th' election**: was chosen

29. **of whom his eyes had seen the proof**: whose ability he had witnessed

31. **be-leed and calmed**: "stopped in my course"

32. **debitor and creditor**: a man who keeps accounts, a contemptuous reference to Cassio's familiarity with books rather than experience; **countercaster**: another term for "accountant"

33. **in good time**: a fine piece of luck for me

34. **ancient**: ensign

38. **letter and affection**: influence and personal liking

39. **gradation**: seniority

41. **affined**: bound by any ties

47. **shall mark**: must notice

Forsooth, a great arithmetician,   20
One Michael Cassio, a Florentine
(A fellow almost damned in a fair wife),
That never set a squadron in the field,
Nor the division of a battle knows
More than a spinster; unless the bookish theoric,   25
Wherein the toged consuls can propose
As masterly as he. Mere prattle, without practice,
Is all his soldiership. But he, sir, had th' election;
And I (of whom his eyes had seen the proof
At Rhodes, at Cyprus, and on other grounds   30
Christian and heathen) must be be-leed and calmed
By debitor and creditor, this counter-caster.
He (in good time!) must his lieutenant be,
And I (God bless the mark!) his Moorship's ancient.
 Rod. By heaven, I rather would have been his hang-   35
  man.
 Iago. Why, there's no remedy; 'tis the curse of service.
Preferment goes by letter and affection,
And not by old gradation, where each second
Stood heir to the first. Now, sir, be judge yourself,   40
Whether I in any just term am affined
To love the Moor.
 Rod.   I would not follow him then.
 Iago. O, sir, content you.
I follow him to serve my turn upon him.   45
We cannot all be masters, nor all masters
Cannot be truly followed. You shall mark
Many a duteous and knee-crooking knave
That, doting on his own obsequious bondage,
Wears out his time, much like his master's ass,   50
For naught but provender; and when he's old, cashiered.

52. **Whip me:** whip, for all I care

53. **trimmed in forms and visages of duty:** suitably but hypocritically simulating duty in their behavior and appearance

56-7. **lined their coats:** lined their pockets

58. **Do themselves homage:** serve themselves (instead of their masters)

61. **Were I the Moor, I would not be Iago:** "since I am Iago it is not to be expected that I will behave with as much devotion to Othello's interests as though I were Othello himself," with the added implication that anyone would prefer to be the master rather than the servant.

62. **follow but myself:** follow my own interest

63-4. **not I for love and duty,/ But seeming so:** I do not act so because of sincere love and duty but only to give that appearance; **peculiar:** personal

66. **act and figure:** functioning and motivation

67. **compliment extern:** external appearance

68. **But:** that

69. **daws:** jackdaws; **I am not what I am:** I am not what I appear to be.

71. **carry't thus:** get away with this

72. **Call up:** that is, from his bed

75-6. **though he in a fertile climate dwell,/ Plague him with flies:** though he is enjoying good luck, plague him with petty irritations.

77. **throw such changes of vexation:** inflict such vexing misadventures

78. **As:** that

80. **timorous accent:** terrifying outcry

3

Whip me such honest knaves! Others there are
Who, trimmed in forms and visages of duty,
Keep yet their hearts attending on themselves;
And, throwing but shows of service on their lords,   55
Do well thrive by them, and when they have lined their
    coats,
Do themselves homage. These fellows have some soul;
And such a one do I profess myself. For, sir,
It is as sure as you are Roderigo,   60
Were I the Moor, I would not be Iago.
In following him, I follow but myself.
Heaven is my judge, not I for love and duty,
But seeming so, for my peculiar end;
For when my outward action doth demonstrate   65
The native act and figure of my heart
In compliment extern, 'tis not long after
But I will wear my heart upon my sleeve
For daws to peck at. I am not what I am.
    Rod. What a full fortune does the thick-lips owe   70
If he can carry't thus!
    Iago.   Call up her father:
Rouse him, make after him, poison his delight,
Proclaim him in the streets, incense her kinsmen,
And though he in a fertile climate dwell,   75
Plague him with flies; though that his joy be joy,
Yet throw such changes of vexation on't
As it may lose some color.
    Rod. Here is her father's house. I'll call aloud.
    Iago. Do, with like timorous accent and dire yell   80
As when, by night and negligence, the fire
Is spied in populous cities.
    Rod. What, ho, Brabantio! Signior Brabantio, ho!

"The description of Venice."
From Fynes Moryson, *Description of Venice* (1617), the travel
diary of an English traveler of the late sixteenth century.

93. **Zounds**: God's wounds
96. **Even now . . . very now**: at this very instant
97. **tupping**: covering
98. **snorting**: snoring
109. **distemp'ring**: intoxicating
110. **Upon**: inspired by
111. **start my quiet**: disturb my peace

Iago. Awake! What, ho, Brabantio! Thieves! thieves!
    thieves!   85
Look to your house, your daughter, and your bags!
Thieves! thieves!

[Enter] *Brabantio* above, at a window.

Bra. What is the reason of this terrible summons?
What is the matter there?
    Rod. Signior, is all your family within?   90
    Iago. Are your doors locked?
    Bra.   Why, wherefore ask you this?
    Iago. Zounds, sir, y'are robbed! For shame, put on
    your gown!
Your heart is burst; you have lost half your soul.   95
Even now, now, very now, an old black ram
Is tupping your white ewe. Arise, arise!
Awake the snorting citizens with the bell,
Or else the devil will make a grandsire of you.
Arise, I say!   100
    Bra.   What, have you lost your wits?
    Rod. Most reverend signior, do you know my voice?
    Bra. Not I. What are you?
    Rod. My name is Roderigo.
    Bra.   The worser welcome!   105
I have charged thee not to haunt about my doors.
In honest plainness thou hast heard me say
My daughter is not for thee; and now, in madness,
Being full of supper and distemp'ring draughts,
Upon malicious knavery dost thou come   110
To start my quiet.
    Rod. Sir, sir, sir—

118. **grange:** isolated farmhouse

126. **gennets:** horses of Spanish breed; **germans:** relations

127. **profane:** foul-mouthed

137. **odd-even . . . watch:** midnight, neither night nor morning

141. **your allowance:** with your knowledge and permission; sanctioned by you

Habito di Gentilhuomo d'estade

A Venetian man of property.
From Giacomo Franco, *Habiti d'huomeni et donne Venetia* (1626).

Bra.   But thou must needs be sure
My spirit and my place have in their power
To make this bitter to thee.   115
    Rod.   Patience, good sir.
    Bra. What tell'st thou me of robbing? This is Venice;
My house is not a grange.
    Rod.   Most grave Brabantio,
In simple and pure soul I come to you.   120
    Iago. Zounds, sir, you are one of those that will not
serve God if the devil bid you. Because we come to do
you service, and you think we are ruffians, you'll have
your daughter covered with a Barbary horse; you'll have
your nephews neigh to you; you'll have coursers for   125
cousins, and gennets for germans.
    Bra. What profane wretch art thou?
    Iago. I am one, sir, that comes to tell you your daugh-
ter and the Moor are now making the beast with two
backs.   130
    Bra. Thou art a villain.
    Iago.   You are a senator.
    Bra. This thou shalt answer. I know thee, Roderigo.
    Rod. Sir, I will answer anything. But I beseech you,
If't be your pleasure and most wise consent   135
(As partly I find it is) that your fair daughter,
At this odd-even and dull watch o' the night,
Transported, with no worse nor better guard
But with a knave of common hire, a gondolier,
To the gross clasps of a lascivious Moor—   140
If this be known to you, and your allowance,
We then have done you bold and saucy wrongs;
But if you know not this, my manners tell me
We have your wrong rebuke. Do not believe

145. **from:** in spite of

148. **gross:** great

150. **extravagant:** (obsolete) "wandering beyond bounds"; **extravagant and wheeling stranger:** a wandering stranger with no fixed place of residence

151. **Straight:** immediately

161. **meet:** fitting; **wholesome to my place:** "healthy" for my job

164. **However this may gall him with some check:** even though he may suffer a reprimand

165. **Cannot:** that is, the state cannot; **cast:** discharge, dismiss

166. **loud:** great, important

168. **fathom:** capacity

174. **Sagittary:** probably a public inn by that name; **raised search:** the men called out to search

That, from the sense of all civility,   145
I thus would play and trifle with your reverence.
Your daughter, if you have not given her leave,
I say again, hath made a gross revolt,
Tying her duty, beauty, wit, and fortunes
In an extravagant and wheeling stranger   150
Of here and everywhere. Straight satisfy yourself.
If she be in her chamber, or your house,
Let loose on me the justice of the state
For thus deluding you.
   Bra.   Strike on the tinder, ho!   155
Give me a taper! Call up all my people!
This accident is not unlike my dream:
Belief of it oppresses me already.
Light, I say! light!   *Exit [above].*
   Iago.   Farewell, for I must leave you.   160
It seems not meet, nor wholesome to my place,
To be produced (as, if I stay, I shall)
Against the Moor. For I do know, the state,
However this may gall him with some check,
Cannot with safety cast him; for he's embarked   165
With such loud reason to the Cyprus wars,
Which even now stand in act, that for their souls
Another of his fathom they have none
To lead their business; in which regard,
Though I do hate him as I do hell pains,   170
Yet, for necessity of present life,
I must show out a flag and sign of love,
Which is indeed but sign. That you shall surely find him,
Lead to the Sagittary the raised search;
And there will I be with him. So farewell.   *Exit.*   175

Venetian gondolas on the canal.
From Giacomo Franco, *Habiti d'huomeni et donne Venetia* (1626).

177. **despised time:** old age

182. **mo:** more

188. **Is there . . . charms:** a singular verb with plural object was common usage.

189. **property:** nature

190. **abused:** deluded

199. **I may command:** my influence is great enough to ensure assistance.

200. **special officers of night:** men specifically appointed to guard the city at night

201. **I'll deserve your pains:** I'll reward your efforts.

Enter, [below,] *Brabantio,* in his nightgown, and *Servants*
with torches.

   Bra. It is too true an evil. Gone she is;
And what's to come of my despised time
Is naught but bitterness. Now, Roderigo,
Where didst thou see her?—O unhappy girl!—
With the Moor, say'st thou?—Who would be a father?— 180
How didst thou know 'twas she?—O, she deceives me
Past thought!—What said she to you?—Get mo tapers!
Raise all my kindred!—Are they married, think you?
   Rod. Truly I think they are.
   Bra. O heaven! How got she out? O treason of the 185
     blood!
Fathers, from hence trust not your daughters' minds
By what you see them act. Is there not charms
By which the property of youth and maidhood
May be abused? Have you not read, Roderigo, 190
Of some such thing?
   Rod.   Yes, sir, I have indeed.
   Bra. Call up my brother.—O, would you had had her!—
Some one way, some another.—Do you know
Where we may apprehend her and the Moor? 195
   Rod. I think I can discover him, if you please
To get good guard and go along with me.
   Bra. Pray you lead on. At every house I'll call;
I may command at most.—Get weapons, ho!
And raise some special officers of night.— 200
On, good Roderigo. I'll deserve your pains.

                                 Exeunt.

I. ii. Iago now slyly warns Othello of Brabantio's rage at the elopement of his daughter. Othello asserts his honest love for Desdemona. Cassio, another object of Iago's hatred, now enters with a summons from the Duke of Venice to Othello calling him to an urgent conference concerning the expedition to Cyprus. At this point, Brabantio comes with his servants to attack Othello, but on news of the Duke's summons he, too, goes to the conference, determined to denounce Othello to the Duke for the use of magic in winning Desdemona.

▪▪▪▪▪▪▪▪▪▪▪▪▪▪▪▪▪▪▪▪▪▪▪▪▪▪▪

2. **very stuff o':** the essence of

5. **yerked:** jabbed

7. **prated:** spoke insolently

8. **scurvy:** uncomplimentary, insulting

11. **I did full hard forbear him:** I could hardly keep from attacking him.

12. **fast:** securely

13. **the magnifico:** Brabantio

14-5. **hath in his effect a voice potential/ As double as the Duke's:** has as much political influence as the Duke himself

17. **enforce it on:** force it to the limit

18. **cable:** rope; i.e., latitude

20. **signiory:** the governing body of Venice

21. **yet to know:** not yet known

24. **demerits:** deserts; no negative meaning as in modern usage

25. **May speak (unbonneted) to:** may face on equal terms, though with due courtesy

Scene II. [Venice. Before the Sagittary.]

Enter *Othello, Iago, Attendants,* with torches.

Iago. Though in the trade of war I have slain men,
Yet do I hold it very stuff o' the conscience
To do no contrived murder. I lack iniquity
Sometimes to do me service. Nine or ten times
I had thought t' have yerked him here under the ribs.   5
   Oth. 'Tis better as it is.
   Iago.   Nay, but he prated,
And spoke such scurvy and provoking terms
Against your honor,
That with the little godliness I have   10
I did full hard forbear him. But I pray you, sir,
Are you fast married? Be assured of this,
That the magnifico is much beloved,
And hath in his effect a voice potential
As double as the Duke's. He will divorce you,   15
Or put upon you what restraint and grievance
The law, with all his might to enforce it on,
Will give him cable.
   Oth.   Let him do his spite.
My services which I have done the signiory   20
Shall out-tongue his complaints. 'Tis yet to know—
Which, when I know that boasting is an honor,
I shall promulgate—I fetch my life and being
From men of royal siege; and my demerits
May speak (unbonneted) to as proud a fortune   25
As this that I have reached. For know, Iago,
But that I love the gentle Desdemona,

A contemporary view of the square before St. Mark's, Venice. From Vecellio, *De gli habiti antichi* (1590).

30. **the sea's worth:** that is, all the treasure buried in the sea

33. **You were best:** it would be best for you to

35. **perfect soul:** clear conscience

37. **Janus:** the double-faced god of Roman mythology

42. **haste-post-haste:** immediate. The phrase was used as a direction for the quick delivery of letters.

47. **sequent:** consecutive

52. **several:** separate

9

I would not my unhoused free condition
Put into circumscription and confine
For the sea's worth.   30

        Enter *Cassio,* and *Officers* with torches.

                  But look what lights come yond.
   Iago. Those are the raised father and his friends.
You were best go in.
     Oth.   Not I. I must be found.
My parts, my title, and my perfect soul   35
Shall manifest me rightly. Is it they?
   Iago. By Janus, I think no.
   Oth. The servants of the Duke? and my lieutenant?
The goodness of the night upon you, friends!
What is the news?   40
     Cas.   The Duke does greet you, General;
And he requires your haste-post-haste appearance
Even on the instant.
     Oth.   What's the matter, think you?
     Cas. Something from Cyprus, as I may divine.   45
It is a business of some heat. The galleys
Have sent a dozen sequent messengers
This very night at one another's heels;
And many of the consuls, raised and met,
Are at the Duke's already. You have been hotly called for; 50
When, being not at your lodging to be found,
The Senate hath sent about three several quests
To search you out.
     Oth.   'Tis well I am found by you.
I will but spend a word here in the house,   55
And go with you.   [*Exit.*]

58. **carrack:** cargo ship
64. **Have with you:** "I'm agreeable; let's go."
66. **be advised:** have a care.
67. **to bad intent:** with bad intent
79. **refer me to:** appeal to

A Venetian officer.
From Giacomo Franco, *Habiti d'huomeni et donne Venetia* (1626).

10

Cas.   Ancient, what makes he here?

Iago. Faith, he tonight hath boarded a land carrack.
If it prove lawful prize, he's made for ever.

Cas. I do not understand.   60

Iago.   He's married.

Cas.   To who?

[Enter *Othello*.]

Iago. Marry, to—Come, Captain, will you go?

Oth.   Have with you.

Cas. Here comes another troop to seek for you.   65

Enter *Brabantio, Roderigo,* and *Officers* with torches
and weapons.

Iago. It is Brabantio. General, be advised;
He comes to bad intent.

Oth.   Holla! stand there!

Rod. Signior, it is the Moor.

Bra.   Down with him, thief!   70
                [*Both parties draw swords.*]

Iago. You, Roderigo! Come, sir, I am for you.

Oth. Keep up your bright swords, for the dew will
    rust them.
Good signior, you shall more command with years
Than with your weapons.   75

Bra. O thou foul thief, where hast thou stowed my
    daughter?
Damned as thou art, thou hast enchanted her!
For I'll refer me to all things of sense,
If she in chains of magic were not bound,   80

86. **fear:** frighten

87. **Judge me the world:** let the world judge for me; **gross in sense:** notably apparent

88. **practiced on:** tricked

89. **Abused:** deceived; see I. i. 190.

90. **motion:** the ability to exercise critical judgment and act accordingly

92. **attach:** arrest

94. **arts inhibited:** forbidden arts; magic; **out of warrant** is synonymous with **inhibited,** that is, "illegal."

100. **Where will you that I go:** where do you wish me to go.

103. **course of direct session:** regular session of court

A Venetian lady and gentleman.
From Fabritio Caroso, *Della nobilita di dame* (1600).

Whether a maid so tender, fair, and happy,
So opposite to marriage that she shunned
The wealthy curled darlings of our nation,
Would ever have (t' incur a general mock)
Run from her guardage to the sooty bosom   85
Of such a thing as thou—to fear, not to delight.
Judge me the world if 'tis not gross in sense
That thou hast practiced on her with foul charms,
Abused her delicate youth with drugs or minerals
That weaken motion. I'll have't disputed on.   90
'Tis probable, and palpable to thinking.
I therefore apprehend and do attach thee
For an abuser of the world, a practicer
Of arts inhibited and out of warrant.
Lay hold upon him. If he do resist,   95
Subdue him at his peril.
   Oth.   Hold your hands,
Both you of my inclining and the rest.
Were it my cue to fight, I should have known it
Without a prompter. Where will you that I go   100
To answer this your charge?
   Bra.   To prison, till fit time
Of law and course of direct session
Call thee to answer.
   Oth.   What if I do obey?   105
How may the Duke be therewith satisfied,
Whose messengers are here about my side
Upon some present business of the state
To bring me to him?
   Officer.   'Tis true, most worthy signior.   110
The Duke's in council, and your noble self,
I am sure, is sent for.

I. iii. At the meeting of the Council, the Duke orders Othello to prepare to sail for Cyprus. On Brabantio's plea for justice, Othello asks that Desdemona be sent for. He tells how he won her heart and hand, and Desdemona confirms his words, pleading to be allowed to accompany him to his post in Cyprus. Brabantio leaves embittered, warning Othello to beware lest Desdemona deceive him as she did her father. Iago is charged with the safe conveyance to Cyprus of Desdemona and her attendant, Emilia, Iago's wife; but alone with Roderigo, who threatens to drown himself, Iago consoles him with promises that he will yet have Desdemona. He assures Roderigo of his hate for Othello, and muses on a plan to arouse Othello to jealousy of the handsome Cassio.

▪▪▪▪▪▪▪▪▪▪▪▪▪▪▪▪▪▪▪▪▪▪▪▪▪▪▪▪

1. **composition**: consistency; **these news**: these reports. **News** was originally considered a plural word.

2. **gives them credit**: makes it possible to credit them

7. **jump not on a just account**: do not agree in reporting the number

8. **the aim**: conjecture

12-4. **I do not so secure me in the error/ But the main article I do approve/ In fearful sense**: the error does not so reassure me that I fail to find the general tenor alarming.

Bra.   How? The Duke in council?
In this time of the night? Bring him away!
Mine's not an idle cause. The Duke himself,   115
Or any of my brothers of the state,
Cannot but feel this wrong as 'twere their own;
For if such actions may have passage free,
Bondslaves and pagans shall our statesmen be.

                                        Exeunt.

Scene III. [Venice. A chamber in the Senate House.]

Enter *Duke* and *Senators,* set at a table, with lights
                    and *Attendants.*

Duke. There is no composition in these news
That gives them credit.
    1. Sen.   Indeed they are disproportioned.
My letters say a hundred and seven galleys.
    Duke. And mine a hundred forty.   5
    2. Sen.   And mine two hundred.
But though they jump not on a just account
(As in these cases where the aim reports
'Tis oft with difference), yet do they all confirm
A Turkish fleet, and bearing up to Cyprus.   10
    Duke. Nay, it is possible enough to judgment.
I do not so secure me in the error
But the main article I do approve
In fearful sense.
    Sailor. (*Within*) What, ho! what, ho! what, ho!   15

21. **How say you by:** what do you say about

22-3. **This cannot be/ By no assay of reason:** "no kind of logic can make this believable." Double negatives were common for emphasis; **pageant:** a mere pretense. Elaborate floats were used in festivities on city streets and on waterways, and the individual floats were called **pageants.**

28. **with more facile question bear it:** take it more easily

29. **For that:** because

33. **latest:** till last

40. **injointed them:** joined

42-3. **re-stem/ Their backward course:** turn their course in the opposite direction

The Duke (Doge) of Venice.
From Giacomo Franco, *Habiti d'huomeni et donne Venetia* (1626).

13

Enter *Sailor*.

Officer. A messenger from the galleys.
Duke.   Now, what's the business?
Sailor. The Turkish preparation makes for Rhodes.
So was I bid report here to the state
By Signior Angelo.   20
Duke. How say you by this change?
1. Sen.   This cannot be
By no assay of reason. 'Tis a pageant
To keep us in false gaze. When we consider
Th' importancy of Cyprus to the Turk,   25
And let ourselves again but understand
That, as it more concerns the Turk than Rhodes,
So may he with more facile question bear it,
For that it stands not in such warlike brace,
But altogether lacks th' abilities   30
That Rhodes is dressed in—if we make thought of this,
We must not think the Turk is so unskilful
To leave that latest which concerns him first,
Neglecting an attempt of ease and gain
To wake and wage a danger profitless.   35
    Duke. Nay, in all confidence he's not for Rhodes.
    Officer. Here is more news.

Enter a *Messenger*.

Mess. The Ottomites, reverend and gracious,
Steering with due course toward the isle of Rhodes,
Have there injointed them with an after fleet.   40
    1. Sen. Ay, so I thought. How many, as you guess?
    Mess. Of thirty sail; and now they do re-stem

A Spanish galley of the seventeenth century.
From Furttenbach's *Architectura navalis* (1629).

46. **With his free duty recommends you thus:**
tenders his unbounded duty in reporting thus

60. **particular:** personal

62. **engluts:** synonymous with **swallows**

69. **mountebanks:** itinerant vendors, so called because they usually stood on benches at fairs or market places to give their "pitch"

Their backward course, bearing with frank appearance
Their purposes toward Cyprus. Signior Montano,
Your trusty and most valiant servitor,   45
With his free duty recommends you thus,
And prays you to believe him.
 Duke. 'Tis certain then for Cyprus.
Marcus Luccicos, is not he in town?
 1. Sen. He's now in Florence.   50
 Duke. Write from us to him; post-post-haste dispatch.

Enter *Brabantio, Othello, Cassio, Iago, Roderigo,*
   and *Officers.*

 1. Sen. Here comes Brabantio and the valiant Moor.
 Duke. Valiant Othello, we must straight employ you
Against the general enemy Ottoman.
[*To Brabantio*] I did not see you. Welcome, gentle signior.   55
We lacked your counsel and your help tonight.
 Bra. So did I yours. Good your Grace, pardon me.
Neither my place, nor aught I heard of business,
Hath raised me from my bed; nor doth the general care
Take hold on me; for my particular grief   60
Is of so floodgate and o'erbearing nature
That it engluts and swallows other sorrows,
And it is still itself.
 Duke.   Why, what's the matter?
 Bra. My daughter! O, my daughter!   65
 All.   Dead?
 Bra.   Ay, to me!
She is abused, stol'n from me, and corrupted
By spells and medicines bought of mountebanks;
For nature so prepost'rously to err,   70

72. **Sans:** without

74. **beguiled . . . of herself:** tricked her out of possession of herself

77. **After your own sense:** according to your interpretation of it; **our proper son:** our son himself

78. **Stood in your action:** were answerable to your grievance

88. **approved good:** demonstrated to be good

94. **pith:** strength

95. **Till now some nine moons wasted:** until nine months ago

96. **dearest:** most intense

101. **round:** plain

Being not deficient, blind, or lame of sense,
Sans witchcraft could not.

  Duke. Whoe'er he be that in this foul proceeding
Hath thus beguiled your daughter of herself,
And you of her, the bloody book of law   75
You shall yourself read in the bitter letter
After your own sense; yea, though our proper son
Stood in your action.

  Bra.   Humbly I thank your Grace.
Here is the man—this Moor, whom now, it seems,   80
Your special mandate, for the state affairs,
Hath hither brought.

  All.   We are very sorry for't.

  Duke. [*To Othello*] What, in your own part, can you
    say to this?   85

  Bra. Nothing, but this is so.

  Oth. Most potent, grave, and reverend signiors,
My very noble, and approved good masters:
That I have ta'en away this old man's daughter,
It is most true; true I have married her.   90
The very head and front of my offending
Hath this extent, no more. Rude am I in my speech,
And little blessed with the soft phrase of peace;
For since these arms of mine had seven years' pith
Till now some nine moons wasted, they have used   95
Their dearest action in the tented field;
And little of this great world can I speak
More than pertains to feats of broil and battle;
And therefore little shall I grace my cause
In speaking for myself. Yet, by your gracious patience,   100
I will a round unvarnished tale deliver
Of my whole course of love—what drugs, what charms,

107. **motion:** critical faculty; see I. ii. 90.

114. **practices:** tricks; see I. ii. 88.

121. **habits:** clothing. The Duke feels that Brabantio's accusations are thinly clothed in mere suppositions.

122. **modern:** ordinary; a usage now obsolete

124. **indirect and forced:** dishonest and unnatural

What conjuration, and what mighty magic
(For such proceeding am I charged withal)
I won his daughter.   105
    Bra.   A maiden never bold;
Of spirit so still and quiet that her motion
Blushed at herself; and she—in spite of nature,
Of years, of country, credit, everything—
To fall in love with what she feared to look on!   110
It is a judgment maimed and most imperfect
That will confess perfection so could err
Against all rules of nature, and must be driven
To find out practices of cunning hell
Why this should be. I therefore vouch again   115
That with some mixtures pow'rful o'er the blood,
Or with some dram, conjured to this effect,
He wrought upon her.
    Duke.   To vouch this is no proof,
Without more certain and more overt test   120
Than these thin habits and poor likelihoods
Of modern seeming do prefer against him.
    1. Sen. But, Othello, speak.
Did you by indirect and forced courses
Subdue and poison this young maid's affections?   125
Or came it by request, and such fair question
As soul to soul affordeth?
    Oth.   I do beseech you,
Send for the lady to the Sagittary
And let her speak of me before her father.   130
If you do find me foul in her report,
The trust, the office, I do hold of you
Not only take away, but let your sentence
Even fall upon my life.

One of the race of men with heads growing beneath their shoulders. From *Livre des Merveilles* (1907), reprinted from a manuscript in the Bibliothèque Nationale.

144. **Still:** continually

154. **portance:** comportment

155. **antres:** a poetic term for caves

158. **hint:** opportunity; **process:** course (of my story)

160. **Anthropophagi:** the Scythians, who, according to travelers' tales, were eaters of human flesh

Duke.   Fetch Desdemona hither.   135
   Oth. Ancient, conduct them; you best know the place.
        Exeunt [Iago and] two or three [Attendants].
And till she come, as truly as to heaven
I do confess the vices of my blood,
So justly to your grave ears I'll present
How I did thrive in this fair lady's love,   140
And she in mine.
   Duke. Say it, Othello.
   Oth. Her father loved me, oft invited me;
Still questioned me the story of my life
From year to year—the battles, sieges, fortunes   145
That I have passed.
I ran it through, even from my boyish days
To the very moment that he bade me tell it.
Wherein I spake of most disastrous chances,
Of moving accidents by flood and field;   150
Of hairbreadth scapes i' th' imminent deadly breach;
Of being taken by the insolent foe
And sold to slavery; of my redemption thence
And portance in my travel's history;
Wherein of antres vast and deserts idle,   155
Rough quarries, rocks, and hills whose heads touch
     heaven,
It was my hint to speak—such was the process;
And of the Cannibals that each other eat,
The Anthropophagi, and men whose heads   160
Do grow beneath their shoulders. This to hear
Would Desdemona seriously incline;
But still the house affairs would draw her thence;
Which ever as she could with haste dispatch,
She'd come again, and with a greedy ear   165

167. **pliant:** convenient

169. **dilate:** relate at length (at one sitting)

170. **by parcels:** bits at a time

171. **intentively:** without distraction

176. **passing:** exceedingly

182. **hint:** opportunity; see I. iii. 158. Othello does not mean that Desdemona gave him a hint in the modern sense to declare himself.

186. **witness:** attest to

189. **Take up this mangled matter at the best:** make the best of this disordered business.

190-91. **Men do their broken weapons rather use/ Than their bare hands:** men, being civilized, prefer weapons, even broken ones, to violence with their bare hands. The Duke is implying that Othello, being a man, would use only methods suitable for a man to gain his ends.

194. **bad:** unjust

Devour up my discourse. Which I observing,
Took once a pliant hour, and found good means
To draw from her a prayer of earnest heart
That I would all my pilgrimage dilate,
Whereof by parcels she had something heard,   170
But not intentively. I did consent,
And often did beguile her of her tears
When I did speak of some distressful stroke
That my youth suffered. My story being done,
She gave me for my pains a world of sighs.   175
She swore, in faith, 'twas strange, 'twas passing strange;
'Twas pitiful, 'twas wondrous pitiful.
She wished she had not heard it; yet she wished
That heaven had made her such a man. She thanked me;
And bade me, if I had a friend that loved her,   180
I should but teach him how to tell my story,
And that would woo her. Upon this hint I spake.
She loved me for the dangers I had passed,
And I loved her that she did pity them.
This only is the witchcraft I have used.   185
Here comes the lady: let her witness it.

Enter *Desdemona, Iago, Attendants.*

Duke. I think this tale would win my daughter too.
Good Brabantio,
Take up this mangled matter at the best.
Men do their broken weapons rather use   190
Than their bare hands.
     Bra.   I pray you hear her speak.
If she confess that she was half the wooer,
Destruction on my head if my bad blame

203. **hitherto your daughter:** that is, before now I was only your daughter.

210. **get:** beget

213. **but thou hast already:** if you did not already have it

214. **For your sake:** on your account

218. **like yourself:** in a manner appropriate to you

219. **grise:** synonymous with **step**

Light on the man! Come hither, gentle mistress.   195
Do you perceive in all this noble company
Where most you owe obedience?
   Des.   My noble father,
I do perceive here a divided duty.
To you I am bound for life and education;   200
My life and education both do learn me
How to respect you: you are the lord of duty;
I am hitherto your daughter. But here's my husband;
And so much duty as my mother showed
To you, preferring you before her father,   205
So much I challenge that I may profess
Due to the Moor my lord.
   Bra.   God be with you! I have done.
Please it your Grace, on to the state affairs.
I had rather to adopt a child than get it.   210
Come hither, Moor.
I here do give thee that with all my heart
Which, but thou hast already, with all my heart
I would keep from thee. For your sake, jewel,
I am glad at soul I have no other child;   215
For thy escape would teach me tyranny,
To hang clogs on them. I have done, my lord.
   Duke. Let me speak like yourself and lay a sentence
Which, as a grise or step, may help these lovers
Into your favor.   220
When remedies are past, the griefs are ended
By seeing the worst, which late on hopes depended.
To mourn a mischief that is past and gone
Is the next way to draw new mischief on.
What cannot be preserved when fortune takes,   225
Patience her injury a mock'ry makes.

228. **bootless:** unavailing

236. **equivocal:** equal

243. **allowed sufficiency:** admitted capability

244. **effects:** results; **throws a more safer voice on you:** acclaims our greater safety under your command

245. **slubber:** dull

246. **stubborn:** dangerous

250-52. **thrice-driven:** three times picked over and sorted to select the best, as was down for pillows; **I do agnize/ A natural and prompt alacrity/ I find in hardness:** I acknowledge my natural and spontaneous readiness to endure hardship.

256. **exhibition:** allowance for subsistence

257. **accommodation and besort:** suitable accommodation

A Turkish "Caramuzzal."
From Furttenbach's *Architectura navalis* (1629).

The robbed that smiles steals something from the thief;
He robs himself that spends a bootless grief.

   Bra. So let the Turk of Cyprus us beguile:
We lose it not, so long as we can smile.   230
He bears the sentence well that nothing bears
But the free comfort which from thence he hears;
But he bears both the sentence and the sorrow
That to pay grief must of poor patience borrow.
These sentences, to sugar, or to gall,   235
Being strong on both sides, are equivocal.
But words are words: I never yet did hear
That the bruised heart was pierced through the ear.
I humbly beseech you, proceed to the affairs of state.

   Duke. The Turk with a most mighty preparation 240
makes for Cyprus. Othello, the fortitude of the place is
best known to you; and though we have there a substi-
tute of most allowed sufficiency, yet opinion, a sovereign
mistress of effects, throws a more safer voice on you.
You must therefore be content to slubber the gloss of your 245
new fortunes with this more stubborn and boist'rous expedition.

   Oth. The tyrant custom, most grave senators,
Hath made the flinty and steel couch of war
My thrice-driven bed of down. I do agnize   250
A natural and prompt alacrity
I find in hardness; and do undertake
These present wars against the Ottomites.
Most humbly, therefore, bending to your state,
I crave fit disposition for my wife;   255
Due reference of place, and exhibition,
With such accommodation and besort
As levels with her breeding.

266. **To my unfolding lend your prosperous ear:** listen to my story with favor.

267-68. **let me find a charter in your voice,/ T' assist my simpleness:** back up my unskilled pleading with your authority.

270. **love the Moor to live with him:** love him because of a wish to share his life

271. **downright violence, and storm of fortunes:** absolutely violent behavior, taking my fortunes by storm (instead of meekly submitting to her father's plans for her life)

272. **subdued:** conquered and altered

273. **quality:** profession (as a soldier)

274. **I saw Othello's visage in his mind:** that is, his qualities overshadowed his physical appearance in my eye.

275. **his honors and his valiant parts:** his reputation and military prowess

278. **A moth:** an idle thing

280. **heavy:** dull, cheerless

282. **voice:** approval

285-86. **heat:** passion; **the young affects/ In my defunct and proper satisfaction:** my newly conceived affection which has not yet been satisfied. (Othello and Desdemona were married earlier on this same evening. Their honeymoon is "defunct," postponed, by state business.)

287. **mind:** wishes

288. **that you think:** against your thinking

290. **For:** because

Duke.   If you please,
Be't at her father's.   260
    Bra.   I'll not have it so.
    Oth. Nor I.
    Des.   Nor would I there reside,
To put my father in impatient thoughts
By being in his eye. Most gracious Duke,   265
To my unfolding lend your prosperous ear,
And let me find a charter in your voice,
T' assist my simpleness.
    Duke. What would you, Desdemona?
    Des. That I did love the Moor to live with him,   270
My downright violence, and storm of fortunes,
May trumpet to the world. My heart's subdued
Even to the very quality of my lord.
I saw Othello's visage in his mind,
And to his honors and his valiant parts   275
Did I my soul and fortunes consecrate.
So that, dear lords, if I be left behind,
A moth of peace, and he go to the war,
The rights for which I love him are bereft me,
And I a heavy interim shall support   280
By his dear absence. Let me go with him.
    Oth. Let her have your voice.
Vouch with me heaven, I therefore beg it not
To please the palate of my appetite,
Nor to comply with heat, the young affects   285
In my defunct and proper satisfaction;
But to be free and bounteous to her mind.
And heaven defend your good souls that you think
I will your serious and great business scant
For she is with me. No, when light-winged toys   290

291. **seel:** close, from French *ciller*, a term from falconry, meaning to sew up the eyelids, as was done to hawks in the taming process

292. **speculative and officed instruments:** eyes (and the critical faculty they influence) which have been detailed for duty

295. **indign:** shameful

296. **Make head:** attack as an armed body; **estimation:** reputation

304-5. **such things else of quality and respect/ As doth import you:** such other things as are appropriate for you to have

308. **conveyance:** escort

314. **delighted:** delightful

Of feathered Cupid seel with wanton dullness
My speculative and officed instruments,
That my disports corrupt and taint my business,
Let housewives make a skillet of my helm,
And all indign and base adversities   295
Make head against my estimation!
   Duke. Be it as you shall privately determine,
Either for her stay or going. Th' affair cries haste,
And speed must answer it. You must away tonight.
   Oth. With all my heart.   300
   Duke. At nine i' th' morning here we'll meet again.
Othello, leave some officer behind,
And he shall our commission bring to you;
With such things else of quality and respect
As doth import you.   305
   Oth.   So please your Grace, my ancient.
A man he is of honesty and trust.
To his conveyance I assign my wife,
With what else needful your good Grace shall think
To be sent after me.   310
   Duke.   Let it be so.
Good night to every one. [*To Brabantio*] And, noble si-
      gnior,
If virtue no delighted beauty lack,
Your son-in-law is far more fair than black.   315
   1. Sen. Adieu, brave Moor. Use Desdemona well.
   Bra. Look to her, Moor, if thou hast eyes to see.
She has deceived her father, and may thee.
           Exit [*with Duke, Senators, Officers, etc.*].
   Oth. My life upon her faith!—Honest Iago,
My Desdemona must I leave to thee.   320
I prithee let thy wife attend on her,

A sixteenth-century ship of war under full sail.
From Olaus Magnus, *Historia de gentibus* (1555).

322. **in the best advantage:** when the best advantage occurs

328. **What will I do, think'st thou:** what do you think I plan to do.

330. **incontinently:** without delay

347. **hyssop:** an aromatic herb

350. **corrigible:** corrective

23

And bring them after in the best advantage.
Come, Desdemona. I have but an hour
Of love, of worldly matters and direction,
To spend with thee. We must obey the time.   325
                    Exeunt Moor and Desdemona.

    Rod. Iago.
    Iago. What say'st thou, noble heart?
    Rod. What will I do, think'st thou?
    Iago. Why, go to bed and sleep.
    Rod. I will incontinently drown myself.   330
    Iago. If thou dost, I shall never love thee after. Why,
thou silly gentleman!
    Rod. It is silliness to live when to live is torment; and
then have we a prescription to die when death is our
physician.   335
    Iago. O villainous! I have looked upon the world for
four times seven years; and since I could distinguish betwixt a benefit and an injury, I never found man that
knew how to love himself. Ere I would say I would drown
myself for the love of a guinea hen, I would change my   340
humanity with a baboon.
    Rod. What should I do? I confess it is my shame to be
so fond, but it is not in my virtue to amend it.
    Iago. Virtue? a fig! 'Tis in ourselves that we are thus
or thus. Our bodies are our gardens, to the which our   345
wills are gardeners; so that if we will plant nettles or sow
lettuce, set hyssop and weed up thyme, supply it with
one gender of herbs or distract it with many—either to
have it sterile with idleness or manured with industry—
why, the power and corrigible authority of this lies in   350
our wills. If the balance of our lives had not one scale of
reason to poise another of sensuality, the blood and base-

355. **unbitted**: uncurbed

356. **sect or scion**: both synonymous for a gráft or cutting

361-62. **perdurable**: imperishable; **stead**: support

363-64. **defeat thy favor with an usurped beard**: spoil your good looks by wearing a false beard (as a disguise)

368. **answerable sequestration**: corresponding separation

369. **wills**: sexual appetites

371. **locusts**: possibly the locust fruit known as St. John's bread

378. **erring**: wandering

381. **clean out of the way**: entirely the wrong course of action

382. **compassing**: achieving

ness of our natures would conduct us to most prepos-
t'rous conclusions. But we have reason to cool our raging
motions, our carnal stings, our unbitted lusts; whereof I 355
take this that you call love to be a sect or scion.

Rod. It cannot be.

Iago. It is merely a lust of the blood and a permission
of the will. Come, be a man! Drown thyself? Drown cats
and blind puppies! I have professed me thy friend, and 360
I confess me knit to thy deserving with cables of perdurable toughness. I could never better stead thee than now.
Put money in thy purse. Follow thou the wars; defeat
thy favor with an usurped beard. I say, put money in
thy purse. It cannot be that Desdemona should long con- 365
tinue her love to the Moor—put money in thy purse—
nor he his to her. It was a violent commencement, and
thou shalt see an answerable sequestration. Put but money
in thy purse. These Moors are changeable in their wills.
Fill thy purse with money. The food that to him now is 370
as luscious as locusts shall be to him shortly as bitter as
coloquintida. She must change for youth. When she is
sated with his body, she will find the error of her choice.
She must have change, she must. Therefore put money
in thy purse. If thou wilt needs damn thyself, do it a 375
more delicate way than drowning. Make all the money
thou canst. If sanctimony and a frail vow betwixt an
erring barbarian and a supersubtle Venetian be not too
hard for my wits and all the tribe of hell, thou shalt enjoy her. Therefore make money. A pox of drowning thy- 380
self! It is clean out of the way. Seek thou rather to be
hanged in compassing thy joy than to be drowned and
go without her.

384. **fast:** firmly attached

388. **is hearted:** comes from the depth of my heart

390. **cuckold him:** make him a cuckold, that is, a betrayed husband

392. **Traverse:** a military term, "about face and march."

396. **betimes:** at an early hour

401. **make my fool my purse:** make my livelihood from some fool

403. **snipe:** fool. The woodcock, or snipe, was easily trapped and the name became a common epithet for a dupe.

405. **thought abroad:** rumored

406. **'Has:** he has; the "he" is elided.

407. **kind:** respect

408. **do as if for surety:** behave as though it were certain; **holds me well:** has a high estimation of me

410. **proper:** handsome

411. **plume up:** glorify

414. **he:** that is, Cassio

415-16. **He hath a person and a smooth dispose/ To be suspected:** his looks and gallant manner make such a suspicion plausible.

Rod. Wilt thou be fast to my hopes, if I depend on the issue? 385

Iago. Thou art sure of me. Go, make money. I have told thee often, and I re-tell thee again and again, I hate the Moor. My cause is hearted; thine hath no less reason. Let us be conjunctive in our revenge against him. If thou canst cuckold him, thou dost thyself a pleasure, me a 390 sport. There are many events in the womb of time, which will be delivered. Traverse! go! provide thy money! We will have more of this tomorrow. Adieu.

Rod. Where shall we meet i' the morning?

Iago. At my lodging. 395

Rod. I'll be with thee betimes.

Iago. Go to, farewell.—Do you hear, Roderigo?

Rod. What say you?

Iago. No more of drowning, do you hear?

Rod. I am changed. I'll go sell all my land.   *Exit.* 400

Iago. Thus do I ever make my fool my purse;
For I mine own gained knowledge should profane
If I would time expend with such a snipe
But for my sport and profit. I hate the Moor;
And it is thought abroad that 'twixt my sheets 405
'Has done my office. I know not if't be true;
Yet I, for mere suspicion in that kind,
Will do as if for surety. He holds me well;
The better shall my purpose work on him.
Cassio's a proper man. Let me see now: 410
To get his place, and to plume up my will
In double knavery—How, how? Let's see.
After some time, to abuse Othello's ear
That he is too familiar with his wife.
He hath a person and a smooth dispose 415

419. **tenderly**: tamely, unresistingly

To be suspected—framed to make women false.
The Moor is of a free and open nature
That thinks men honest that but seem to be so,
And will as tenderly be led by the nose
As asses are.   420
I have't! It is engend'red! Hell and night
Must bring this monstrous birth to the world's light.

Exit.

THE TRAGEDY OF
OTHELLO,
THE MOOR OF VENICE

ACT II

II. i. The Turkish fleet, sailing to attack Cyprus, is destroyed by a storm. Othello, Desdemona, and other members of the Venetian group land safely. Iago observes Cassio with Desdemona and points out to Roderigo how plausible it is that Desdemona should prefer such a courtly and presentable young man to Othello. He outlines to Roderigo a plan to provoke Cassio to a quarrel and lose him his commission as the first step toward gaining Roderigo's wish (Desdemona) and his own (revenge on Othello and Cassio).

᠃᠃᠃᠃᠃᠃᠃᠃᠃᠃᠃᠃᠃᠃᠃᠃᠃᠃᠃᠃

9. **hold the mortise:** hold at the joints
10. **segregation:** scattering
12. **chidden:** assailed (by the wind)
14. **burning Bear:** the constellation, Ursa Minor
15. **Guards of th' ever-fixed pole:** two bright stars in Ursa Minor on a line with the Pole Star
16. **I never did like molestation view:** I never saw a similar commotion.
17. **enchafed:** angry, raging
18. **If that:** if

ACT II

Scene I. [A seaport in Cyprus. An open place
near the harbor.]

Enter Montano and two Gentlemen.

Mon. What from the cape can you discern at sea?
1. Gent. Nothing at all, it is a high-wrought flood;
I cannot 'twixt the heaven and the main
Descry a sail.
Mon. Methinks the wind hath spoke aloud at land;   5
A fuller blast ne'er shook our battlements.
If it hath ruffianed so upon the sea,
What ribs of oak, when mountains melt on them,
Can hold the mortise? What shall we hear of this?
2. Gent. A segregation of the Turkish fleet.   10
For do but stand upon the foaming shore,
The chidden billow seems to pelt the clouds;
The wind-shaked surge, with high and monstrous mane,
Seems to cast water on the burning Bear
And quench the Guards of th' ever-fixed pole.   15
I never did like molestation view
On the enchafed flood.
Mon.   If that the Turkish fleet

20. **bear it out:** ride out the storm

24. **sufferance:** disaster

28. **A Veronesa:** a ship from Verona, though in the service of Venice

47. **arrivance:** a collective word, arrivals

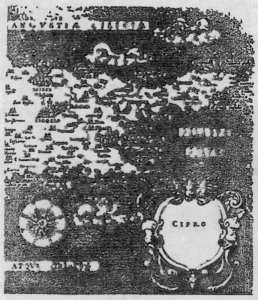

A map of Cyprus.
From T. Porcacchi, *L'isole piu famose* (1590).

Be not ensheltered and embayed, they are drowned.
It is impossible they bear it out.   20

Enter a third *Gentleman.*

    3. Gent. News, lads! Our wars are done.
The desperate tempest hath so banged the Turks
That their designment halts. A noble ship of Venice
Hath seen a grievous wrack and sufferance
On most part of their fleet.   25
    Mon. How? Is this true?
    3. Gent.   The ship is here put in,
A Veronesa; Michael Cassio,
Lieutenant to the warlike Moor Othello,
Is come on shore; the Moor himself at sea,   30
And is in full commission here for Cyprus.
    Mon. I am glad on't. 'Tis a worthy governor.
    3. Gent. But this same Cassio, though he speak of
        comfort
Touching the Turkish loss, yet he looks sadly   35
And prays the Moor be safe, for they were parted
With foul and violent tempest.
    Mon.   Pray heaven he be;
For I have served him, and the man commands
Like a full soldier. Let's to the seaside, ho!   40
As well to see the vessel that's come in
As to throw out our eyes for brave Othello,
Even till we make the main and th' aerial blue
An indistinct regard.
    3. Gent.   Come, let's do so;   45
For every minute is expectancy
Of more arrivance.

54. **approved allowance**: demonstrated ability

55-6. **my hopes (not surfeited to death)/ Stand in bold cure**: Cassio refers obliquely to a Biblical saying in Prov. 13: 12: "hope deferred maketh the heart sick." His hopes are newly conceived and therefore not yet to be despaired of.

68. **achieved**: won

69. **paragons**: surpasses; **wild fame**: exaggerated rumor

70. **quirks**: fanciful expressions; **blazoning**: praising

71-2. **in th' essential vesture of creation/ Does tire the ingener**: her natural endowments are so superlative that one who tries to praise her is wearied with the effort of saying enough. Ingener means "engineer," that is, "contriver."

A sixteenth-century sea battle.
From Olaus Magnus, *Historia de gentibus* (1555).

Enter *Cassio.*

Cas. Thanks you, the valiant of this warlike isle,
That so approve the Moor! O, let the heavens
Give him defense against the elements,   50
For I have lost him on a dangerous sea!
   Mon. Is he well shipped?
   Cas. His bark is stoutly timbered, and his pilot
Of very expert and approved allowance.
Therefore my hopes (not surfeited to death)   55
Stand in bold cure.

                (Within) "A sail, a sail, a sail!"

Enter a *Messenger.*

   Cas. What noise?
   Mess. The town is empty; on the brow o' the sea
Stand ranks of people, and they cry "A sail!"   60
   Cas. My hopes do shape him for the Governor.

                           A shot.
   2. Gent. They do discharge their shot of courtesy.
Our friends at least.
   Cas.   I pray you, sir, go forth
And give us truth who 'tis that is arrived.   65
   2. Gent. I shall.   *Exit.*
   Mon. But, good Lieutenant, is your general wived?
   Cas. Most fortunately. He hath achieved a maid
That paragons description and wild fame;
One that excels the quirks of blazoning pens,   70
And in th' essential vesture of creation
Does tire the ingener.

78. **ensteeped:** sunken
79. **omit:** forgo
80. **mortal:** deadly
85. **footing:** landing
86. **se'nnight's:** that is, a week's
88. **tall:** fine
90. **extincted:** quenched

Enter Second Gentleman.

               How now? Who has put in?
  2. Gent. 'Tis one Iago, ancient to the General.
  Cas. Has had most favorable and happy speed.   75
Tempests themselves, high seas, and howling winds,
The guttered rocks and congregated sands,
Traitors ensteeped to clog the guiltless keel,
As having sense of beauty, do omit
Their mortal natures, letting go safely by   80
The divine Desdemona.
  Mon.   What is she?
  Cas. She that I spake of, our great captain's captain,
Left in the conduct of the bold Iago,
Whose footing here anticipates our thoughts   85
A se'nnight's speed. Great Jove, Othello guard,
And swell his sail with thine own pow'rful breath,
That he may bless this bay with his tall ship,
Make love's quick pants in Desdemona's arms,
Give renewed fire to our extincted spirits,   90
And bring all Cyprus comfort!

Enter Desdemona, Iago, Roderigo, and Emilia [with
Attendants].

                  O, behold!
The riches of the ship is come on shore!
You men of Cyprus, let her have your knees.
Hail to thee, lady! and the grace of heaven,   95
Before, behind thee, and on every hand,
Enwheel thee round!

120. **I find it still**: I find it ever active; **I have list**: I wish

125. **pictures out of doors**: pretty as pictures away from home (when on public view)

126. **bells in your parlors**: that is, with voices as musical as bells when acting the hostess

128. **Players**: triflers; **housewives**: hussies, wantons

A "wildcat in her kitchen."
From the Trevelyon MS. in the Folger Shakespeare Library.

Des. I thank you, valiant Cassio.
What tidings can you tell me of my lord?

Cas. He is not yet arrived; nor know I aught 100
But that he's well and will be shortly here.

Des. O, but I fear! How lost you company?

Cas. The great contention of the sea and skies
Parted our fellowship.

      (Within) "A sail, a sail!" [*A shot.*] 105
      But hark. A sail!

2. Gent. They give their greeting to the citadel.
This likewise is a friend.

Cas.   See for the news.
       [*Exit Gentleman.*]

Good ancient, you are welcome. [*To Emilia*] Welcome, 110
 mistress.
Let it not gall your patience, good Iago,
That I extend my manners. 'Tis my breeding
That gives me this bold show of courtesy. [*Kisses her.*]

Iago. Sir, would she give you so much of her lips 115
As of her tongue she oft bestows on me,
You would have enough.

Des.   Alas, she has no speech!

Iago. In faith, too much.
I find it still when I have list to sleep. 120
Marry, before your ladyship, I grant,
She puts her tongue a little in her heart
And chides with thinking.

Emil. You have little cause to say so.

Iago. Come on, come on! You are pictures out of doors, 125
Bells in your parlors, wildcats in your kitchens,
Saints in your injuries, devils being offended,
Players in your housewifery, and housewives in your beds.

138. **assay:** make an effort

143-44. **my invention/ Comes from my pate as birdlime does from frieze: birdlime** was a sticky concoction used to trap birds; **frieze,** a cloth with a heavy nap. Iago pretends to a halting imagination.

148. **The one's for use, the other useth it:** that is, her wit uses her beauty for her advantage.

149. **black:** uncomely. Fairness was a standard of beauty in Elizabethan times.

151. **white:** a pun on "wight," fellow, may be intended. "If she is ugly and yet is clever, she'll find a lover who will be pleased with her."

157. **fond:** foolish

Des. O, fie upon thee, slanderer!

Iago. Nay, it is true, or else I am a Turk.   130
You rise to play, and go to bed to work.

Emil. You shall not write my praise.

Iago.   No, let me not.

Des. What wouldst thou write of me, if thou shouldst
      praise me?   135

Iago. O gentle lady, do not put me to't,
For I am nothing if not critical.

Des. Come on, assay.—There's one gone to the harbor?

Iago. Ay, madam.

Des. I am not merry; but I do beguile   140
The thing I am by seeming otherwise.
Come, how wouldst thou praise me?

Iago. I am about it; but indeed my invention
Comes from my pate as birdlime does from frieze—
It plucks out brains and all. But my Muse labors,   145
And thus she is delivered:

      If she be fair and wise, fairness and wit—
      The one's for use, the other useth it.

Des. Well praised! How if she be black and witty?

Iago. If she be black, and thereto have a wit,   150
      She'll find a white that shall her black-
            ness fit.

Des. Worse and worse!

Emil. How if fair and foolish?

Iago. She never yet was foolish that was fair,   155
      For even her folly helped her to an heir.

Des. These are old fond paradoxes to make fools

159. **foul:** ugly

165-66. **a deserving woman indeed:** a woman who really deserves praise; **in the authority of:** by virtue of

167. **justly put on the vouch of very malice itself:** rightly claim the approval of even the most malicious

169. **Had tongue at will:** was able to express herself when she wished

172. **gay:** richly dressed

180-81. **change the cod's head for the salmon's tail:** that is, in no exchange would she swap a better for a less desirable object.

laugh i' th' alehouse. What miserable praise hast thou
for her that's foul and foolish?

Iago. There's none so foul, and foolish there-   160
    unto,
    But does foul pranks which fair and
      wise ones do.

Des. O heavy ignorance! Thou praisest the worst
best. But what praise couldst thou bestow on a deserving 165
woman indeed—one that, in the authority of her merit,
did justly put on the vouch of very malice itself?

Iago. She that was ever fair, and never proud;
    Had tongue at will, and yet was never
      loud;   170
    Never lacked gold, and yet went never
      gay;
    Fled from her wish, and yet said "Now
      I may";
    She that, being angered, her revenge   175
      being nigh,
    Bade her wrong stay, and her displeas-
      ure fly;
    She that in wisdom never was so frail
    To change the cod's head for the salm-   180
      on's tail;
    She that could think, and ne'er disclose
      her mind;
    See suitors following, and not look
      behind: 185
    She was a wight (if ever such wight
      were)—

189. **chronicle small beer:** keep household accounts
192. **liberal:** licentious
194. **speaks home:** drives home a blunt truth
199. **gyve:** fetter
201-2. **kissed your three fingers:** a gallant gesture
204. **curtsy:** courtesy
205. **clyster:** syringe for enema

Des. To do what?

Iago. To suckle fools and chronicle small beer.

Des. O most lame and impotent conclusion! Do not 190
learn of him, Emilia, though he be thy husband. How
say you, Cassio? Is he not a most profane and liberal
counsellor?

Cas. He speaks home, madam. You may relish him
more in the soldier than in the scholar. 195

Iago. [*Aside*] He takes her by the palm. Ay, well
said, whisper! With as little a web as this will I ensnare
as great a fly as Cassio. Ay, smile upon her, do! I will
gyve thee in thine own courtship. You say true; 'tis so,
indeed! If such tricks as these strip you out of your 200
lieutenantry, it had been better you had not kissed your
three fingers so oft—which now again you are most apt
to play the sir in. Very good! well kissed! an excellent
curtsy! 'Tis so, indeed. Yet again your fingers to your
lips? Would they were clyster pipes for your sake! 205
(*Trumpet within*) The Moor! I know his trumpet.

Cas. 'Tis truly so.

Des. Let's meet him and receive him.

Cas. Lo, where he comes!

Enter *Othello* and *Attendants.*

Oth. O my fair warrior! 210
Des.   My dear Othello!
Oth. It gives me wonder great as my content
To see you here before me. O my soul's joy!
If after every tempest come such calms,
May the winds blow till they have wakened death! 215

218-19. If it were now to die,/ 'Twere now to be most happy: if I died at this moment, it would be at the peak of my happiness.

221. comfort: delight

222. Succeeds: follows

232. set down the pegs that make this music: that is, untune you, as the tune of a stringed instrument would be altered by slackening the strings

233. As honest as I am: an ironic reference to the fact that he is repeatedly called honest by the chief characters of the play

237. desired: loved

239-40. out of fashion: unsuitably; **dote/ In:** behave foolishly on account of

And let the laboring bark climb hills of seas
Olympus-high, and duck again as low
As hell's from heaven! If it were now to die,
'Twere now to be most happy; for I fear
My soul hath her content so absolute   220
That not another comfort like to this
Succeeds in unknown fate.

  Des.   The heavens forbid
But that our loves and comforts should increase
Even as our days do grow!   225

  Oth.   Amen to that, sweet powers!
I cannot speak enough of this content;
It stops me here; it is too much of joy.
And this, and this, the greatest discords be

                       They kiss.

That e'er our hearts shall make!   230

  Iago.   [*Aside*] O, you are well tuned now!
But I'll set down the pegs that make this music,
As honest as I am.

  Oth.   Come, let us to the castle.
News, friends! Our wars are done; the Turks are drowned. 235
How does my old acquaintance of this isle?—
Honey, you shall be well desired in Cyprus;
I have found great love amongst them. O my sweet,
I prattle out of fashion, and I dote
In mine own comforts. I prithee, good Iago,   240
Go to the bay and disembark my coffers.
Bring thou the master to the citadel.
He is a good one, and his worthiness
Does challenge much respect.—Come, Desdemona,
Once more well met at Cyprus.   245

               Exeunt [all but Iago and Roderigo].

253. **Lay thy finger thus:** that is, on your mouth; speak not.

261. **favor:** face

265. **Very:** mere

267. **pregnant and unforced:** readily apparent and natural

269. **voluble:** fluent in expressing insincere gallantries

270. **conscionable:** conscientious

271, 272. **salt, loose:** lecherous

273. **slipper:** slippery

274. **stamp and counterfeit:** contrive to see

277. **green:** inexperienced

Iago. Do thou meet me presently at the harbor. Come hither. If thou be'st valiant (as they say base men being in love have then a nobility in their natures more than is native to them), list me. The Lieutenant tonight watches on the court of guard. First, I must tell thee this: Desdemona is directly in love with him. 250

Rod. With him? Why, 'tis not possible.

Iago. Lay thy finger thus, and let thy soul be instructed. Mark me with what violence she first loved the Moor, but for bragging and telling her fantastical lies; 255 and will she love him still for prating? Let not thy discreet heart think it. Her eye must be fed; and what delight shall she have to look on the devil? When the blood is made dull with the act of sport, there should be, again to inflame it and to give satiety a fresh appetite, 260 loveliness in favor, sympathy in years, manners, and beauties; all which the Moor is defective in. Now for want of these required conveniences, her delicate tenderness will find itself abused, begin to heave the gorge, disrelish and abhor the Moor. Very nature will instruct 265 her in it and compel her to some second choice. Now, sir, this granted (as it is a most pregnant and unforced position), who stands so eminent in the degree of this fortune as Cassio does? A knave very voluble; no further conscionable than in putting on the mere form of civil 270 and humane seeming for the better compass of his salt and most hidden loose affection? Why, none! why, none! A slipper and subtle knave; a finder of occasion; that has an eye can stamp and counterfeit advantages, though true advantage never present itself; a devilish knave! Be- 275 sides, the knave is handsome, young, and hath all those requisites in him that folly and green minds look after.

282-83. **The wine she drinks is made of grapes:** that is, she is human (and capable of human error).

291. **mutualities:** reciprocal courtesies; **marshal:** usher

297. **tainting:** discrediting

299. **minister:** dictate

302. **haply:** perhaps; **truncheon:** baton of office

304-5. **whose qualification shall come into no true taste:** who will not be satisfied

307. **prefer:** further

A pestilent complete knave! and the woman hath found him already.

Rod. I cannot believe that in her. She's full of most 280 blessed condition.

Iago. Blessed fig's-end! The wine she drinks is made of grapes. If she had been blessed, she would never have loved the Moor. Blessed pudding! Didst thou not see her paddle with the palm of his hand? Didst not mark that? 285

Rod. Yes, that I did; but that was but courtesy.

Iago. Lechery, by this hand! an index and obscure prologue to the history of lust and foul thoughts. They met so near with their lips that their breaths embraced together. Villainous thoughts, Roderigo! When these 290 mutualities so marshal the way, hard at hand comes the master and main exercise, th' incorporate conclusion. Pish! But, sir, be you ruled by me. I have brought you from Venice. Watch you tonight; for the command, I'll lay't upon you. Cassio knows you not. I'll not be far 295 from you. Do you find some occasion to anger Cassio, either by speaking too loud, or tainting his discipline, or from what other course you please which the time shall more favorably minister.

Rod. Well.   300

Iago. Sir, he is rash and very sudden in choler, and haply with his truncheon may strike at you. Provoke him that he may; for even out of that will I cause these of Cyprus to mutiny; whose qualification shall come into no true taste again but by the displanting of Cassio. 305 So shall you have a shorter journey to your desires by the means I shall then have to prefer them; and the impediment most profitably removed without the which there were no expectation of our prosperity.

315. **of great credit:** easy to believe

322. **diet:** feed

328. **yet that:** till

331-32. **whom I trace/ For his quick hunting:** whose footsteps I dog to make him hunt more quickly. Iago finds Roderigo too easily discouraged and in need of constant prompting; **stand the putting on:** that is, carry through the plan to provoke a quarrel with Cassio

333. **on the hip:** at a disadvantage, a wrestling term

334. **garb:** manner

337. **egregiously:** to an extraordinary degree

338. **practicing upon:** plotting against

339. **'Tis here, but yet confused:** that is, the potentialities of the situation are great, though my plan is not completed in detail.

A pestilent complete knave! and the woman hath found
him already.

Rod. I cannot believe that in her. She's full of most 280
blessed condition.

Iago. Blessed fig's-end! The wine she drinks is made of
grapes. If she had been blessed, she would never have
loved the Moor. Blessed pudding! Didst thou not see her
paddle with the palm of his hand? Didst not mark that? 285

Rod. Yes, that I did; but that was but courtesy.

Iago. Lechery, by this hand! an index and obscure
prologue to the history of lust and foul thoughts. They
met so near with their lips that their breaths embraced
together. Villainous thoughts, Roderigo! When these 290
mutualities so marshal the way, hard at hand comes the
master and main exercise, th' incorporate conclusion.
Pish! But, sir, be you ruled by me. I have brought you
from Venice. Watch you tonight; for the command, I'll
lay't upon you. Cassio knows you not. I'll not be far 295
from you. Do you find some occasion to anger Cassio,
either by speaking too loud, or tainting his discipline, or
from what other course you please which the time shall
more favorably minister.

Rod. Well. 300

Iago. Sir, he is rash and very sudden in choler, and
haply with his truncheon may strike at you. Provoke
him that he may; for even out of that will I cause these
of Cyprus to mutiny; whose qualification shall come into
no true taste again but by the displanting of Cassio. 305
So shall you have a shorter journey to your desires by
the means I shall then have to prefer them; and the
impediment most profitably removed without the which
there were no expectation of our prosperity.

315. **of great credit:** easy to believe

322. **diet:** feed

328. **yet that:** till

331-32. **whom I trace/ For his quick hunting:** whose footsteps I dog to make him hunt more quickly. Iago finds Roderigo too easily discouraged and in need of constant prompting; **stand the putting on:** that is, carry through the plan to provoke a quarrel with Cassio

333. **on the hip:** at a disadvantage, a wrestling term

334. **garb:** manner

337. **egregiously:** to an extraordinary degree

338. **practicing upon:** plotting against

339. **'Tis here, but yet confused:** that is, the potentialities of the situation are great, though my plan is not completed in detail.

    Rod. I will do this if I can bring it to any opportunity. 310
    Iago. I warrant thee. Meet me by-and-by at the citadel.
I must fetch his necessaries ashore. Farewell.
    Rod. Adieu.   *Exit.*
    Iago. That Cassio loves her, I do well believe it;
That she loves him, 'tis apt and of great credit.   315
The Moor (howbeit that I endure him not)
Is of a constant, loving, noble nature,
And I dare think he'll prove to Desdemona
A most dear husband. Now I do love her too;
Not out of absolute lust (though peradventure   320
I stand accountant for as great a sin)
But partly led to diet my revenge,
For that I do suspect the lusty Moor
Hath leaped into my seat; the thought whereof
Doth, like a poisonous mineral, gnaw my inwards;   325
And nothing can or shall content my soul
Till I am evened with him, wife for wife;
Or failing so, yet that I put the Moor
At least into a jealousy so strong
That judgment cannot cure. Which thing to do   330
If this poor trash of Venice, whom I trace
For his quick hunting, stand the putting on,
I'll have our Michael Cassio on the hip,
Abuse him to the Moor in the right garb
(For I fear Cassio with my nightcap too),   335
Make the Moor thank me, love me, and reward me
For making him egregiously an ass
And practicing upon his peace and quiet
Even to madness. 'Tis here, but yet confused.
Knavery's plain face is never seen till used.   340
                                  Exit.

II. ii.

3. **mere perdition:** complete destruction
8. **offices:** the rooms from which food and drink are dispensed

        ▬▬▬▬▬▬▬▬▬▬▬▬▬▬▬

II. [iii.] Iago contrives to make Cassio drunk and involves him in a brawl that brings Othello to investigate. At the sight of his lieutenant drunk and fighting while supposedly in command of the watch, Othello discharges him. Iago advises Cassio to seek Desdemona's aid in persuading Othello to restore his commission. Iago intends to make Othello believe that Desdemona pleads for Cassio because of guilty love for him.

Scene II. [Cyprus. Before Othello's Castle.]

Enter *Othello's Herald,* with a proclamation; [people
following].

Her. It is Othello's pleasure, our noble and valiant
general, that, upon certain tidings now arrived, importing
the mere perdition of the Turkish fleet, every man put
himself into triumph; some to dance, some to make bon-
fires, each man to what sport and revels his addiction   5
leads him. For, besides these beneficial news, it is the
celebration of his nuptial. So much was his pleasure
should be proclaimed. All offices are open, and there is
full liberty of feasting from this present hour of five till
the bell have told eleven. Heaven bless the isle of Cyprus   10
and our noble general Othello!

Exeunt.

[Scene III. Cyprus. Within the Castle.]

Enter *Othello, Desdemona, Cassio,* and *Attendants.*

Oth. Good Michael, look you to the guard tonight.
Let's teach ourselves that honorable stop,
Not to outsport discretion.
    Cas. Iago hath direction what to do;
But notwithstanding, with my personal eye   5
Will I look to't.

14. **Not this hour:** not for another hour
15. **cast:** dismissed; see I. i. 165.
28. **stoup:** a large cup or tankard
29. **fain:** gladly; **measure:** draught

Oth.   Iago is most honest.
Michael, good night. Tomorrow with your earliest
Let me have speech with you.—Come, my dear love.
The purchase made, the fruits are to ensue;   10
That profit's yet to come 'tween me and you.—
Good night.

> *Exeunt Othello and Desdemona [with Attendants].*

> Enter *Iago.*

Cas. Welcome, Iago. We must to the watch.
Iago. Not this hour, Lieutenant; 'tis not yet ten o' the
clock. Our general cast us thus early for the love of his   15
Desdemona; who let us not therefore blame. He hath not
yet made wanton the night with her, and she is sport for
Jove.
Cas. She's a most exquisite lady.
Iago. And I'll warrant her, full of game.   20
Cas. Indeed, she's a most fresh and delicate creature.
Iago. What an eye she has! Methinks it sounds a
parley to provocation.
Cas. An inviting eye; and yet methinks right modest.
Iago. And when she speaks, is it not an alarum to love?   25
Cas. She is indeed perfection.
Iago. Well, happiness to their sheets! Come, Lieu-
tenant, I have a stoup of wine, and here without are a
brace of Cyprus gallants that would fain have a measure
to the health of black Othello.   30
Cas. Not tonight, good Iago. I have very poor and unhappy brains for drinking. I could well wish courtesy
would invent some other custom of entertainment.

34-5. **I'll drink for you**: that is, when a toast is proposed. It was the custom for each man to respond to a toast by draining his tankard.

37. **qualified**: diluted; **innovation**: change, referring to the fact that he is already a little flushed

44. **dislikes**: displeases

50-1. **caroused/ Potations pottle-deep**: he has emptied his tankard (a pottle) in numerous toasts.

52. **swelling**: majestic

53. **hold their honors in a wary distance**: are quick to take offense on the grounds of honor

54. **very elements**: that is, in their quickness to quarrel they reflect the state of war in Cyprus.

55. **flustered**: confused with drink

60. **If consequence do but approve my dream**: if the result only confirms my expectation

Iago. O, they are our friends. But one cup! I'll drink
for you.   35

Cas. I have drunk but one cup tonight, and that was
craftily qualified too; and behold what innovation it
makes here. I am unfortunate in the infirmity and dare
not task my weakness with any more.

Iago. What, man! 'Tis a night of revels. The gallants   40
desire it.

Cas. Where are they?

Iago. Here at the door. I pray you call them in.

Cas. I'll do't, but it dislikes me.   *Exit.*

Iago. If I can fasten but one cup upon him   45
With that which he hath drunk tonight already,
He'll be as full of quarrel and offense
As my young mistress' dog. Now my sick fool Roderigo,
Whom love hath turned almost the wrong side out,
To Desdemona hath tonight caroused   50
Potations pottle-deep; and he's to watch.
Three lads of Cyprus—noble swelling spirits,
That hold their honors in a wary distance,
The very elements of this warlike isle—
Have I tonight flustered with flowing cups,   55
And they watch too. Now, 'mongst this flock of drunkards
Am I to put our Cassio in some action
That may offend the isle.

Enter *Cassio, Montano,* and *Gentlemen;* [*Servant* with
wine].

                    But here they come.
If consequence do but approve my dream,   60
My boat sails freely, both with wind and stream.

A drinking bout.
From a seventeenth-century illustration to a popular ballad.

62. **rouse:** a deep draught

79. **sweats not to overthrow your Almain:** has little difficulty in surpassing a German

82. **do you justice:** match your toast

84-91. **King Stephen, etc.:** a well-known song, "Bell My Wife"; **lown:** lout; **'Tis pride that pulls the country down:** that is, pride which leads to expensive dress disrupts the country's finances.

Cas. Fore God, they have given me a rouse already.

Mon. Good faith, a little one; not past a pint, as I am a
soldier.

Iago. Some wine, ho!   65

[*Sings*]

> And let me the canakin clink, clink;
> And let me the canakin clink.
> > A soldier's a man;
> > A life's but a span,
> Why then, let a soldier drink.   70

Some wine, boys!

Cas. Fore God, an excellent song!

Iago. I learned it in England, where indeed they are
most potent in potting. Your Dane, your German, and
your swag-bellied Hollander—Drink, ho!—are nothing to   75
your English.

Cas. Is your Englishman so expert in his drinking?

Iago. Why, he drinks you with facility your Dane dead
drunk; he sweats not to overthrow your Almain; he gives
your Hollander a vomit ere the next pottle can be filled.   80

Cas. To the health of our General!

Mon. I am for it, Lieutenant, and I'll do you justice.

Iago. O sweet England!

[*Sings*]

> King Stephen was and a worthy peer;
> > His breeches cost him but a crown;   85
> He held 'em sixpence all too dear,
> > With that he called the tailor lown.
> He was a wight of high renown,
> > And thou art but of low degree.

113. **platform:** location of the guard on watch
118. **equinox:** equivalent
119. **'Tis pity of him:** it's a pity about him.

'Tis pride that pulls the country down; 90
Then take thine auld cloak about thee.

Some wine, ho!

Cas. Fore God, this is a more exquisite song than the other.

Iago. Will you hear't again? 95

Cas. No, for I hold him unworthy of his place that does those things. Well, God's above all; and there be souls must be saved, and there be souls must not be saved.

Iago. It's true, good Lieutenant.

Cas. For mine own part—no offense to the General, nor 100 any man of quality—I hope to be saved.

Iago. And so do I too, Lieutenant.

Cas. Ay, but, by your leave, not before me. The lieutenant is to be saved before the ancient. Let's have no more of this; let's to our affairs. God forgive us our sins! 105 Gentlemen, let's look to our business. Do not think, gentlemen, I am drunk. This is my ancient. This is my right hand, and this is my left. I am not drunk now. I can stand well enough, and speak well enough.

All. Excellent well! 110

Cas. Why, very well then. You must not think then that I am drunk. *Exit.*

Mon. To the platform, masters. Come, let's set the
watch.

Iago. You see this fellow that is gone before. 115
He is a soldier fit to stand by Cæsar
And give direction; and do but see his vice.
'Tis to his virtue a just equinox,
The one as long as th' other. 'Tis pity of him.
I fear the trust Othello puts him in, 120

121. **On**: at
125. **horologe**: clock; **a double set**: twenty-four hours
127. **It were**: it would be
136. **engraffed**: deeply engrained

On some odd time of his infirmity,
Will shake this island.
    Mon.   But is he often thus?
    Iago. 'Tis evermore the prologue to his sleep.
He'll watch the horologe a double set   125
If drink rock not his cradle.
    Mon.   It were well
The General were put in mind of it.
Perhaps he sees it not, or his good nature
Prizes the virtue that appears in Cassio   130
And looks not on his evils. Is not this true?

Enter Roderigo.

    Iago. [*Aside to him*] How now, Roderigo?
I pray you after the Lieutenant, go!   *Exit Roderigo.*
    Mon. And 'tis great pity that the noble Moor
Should hazard such a place as his own second   135
With one of an engraffed infirmity.
It were an honest action to say
So to the Moor.
    Iago.   Not I, for this fair island!
I do love Cassio well and would do much   140
To cure him of this evil.
                  (*Within*) "Help! Help!"
                 But hark! What noise?

Enter Cassio, driving in Roderigo.

    Cas. Zounds, you rogue! you rascal!
    Mon. What's the matter, Lieutenant?   145

147. **twiggen bottle:** a bottle covered with a woven covering, like a Chianti bottle. Cassio threatens to beat Roderigo so unmercifully that he will seek safety even if he has to crawl into a bottle, the only hiding place available.

153. **mazzard:** slang for head

Cas.   A knave teach me my duty?
I'll beat the knave into a twiggen bottle.
   Rod. Beat me?
   Cas.   Dost thou prate, rogue?   [*Strikes him.*]
   Mon.   Nay, good Lieutenant! 150
                              [*Takes his arm.*]
I pray you, sir, hold your hand.
   Cas.   Let me go, sir,
Or I'll knock you o'er the mazzard.
   Mon.   Come, come, you're drunk!
   Cas. Drunk?   *They fight.* 155
   Iago. [*Aside to Roderigo*] Away, I say! Go out and cry
     a mutiny!

                          Exit Roderigo.
Nay, good Lieutenant. God's will, gentlemen!
Help, ho!—Lieutenant—sir—Montano—sir—
Help, masters!—Here's a goodly watch indeed!   160
                          A bell rung.
Who's that which rings the bell? Diablo, ho!
The town will rise. God's will, Lieutenant, hold!
You will be shamed for ever.

          Enter *Othello* and *Attendants.*

   Oth.   What is the matter here?
   Mon. I bleed still. I am hurt to the death. He dies! 165
   Oth. Hold for your lives!
   Iago. Hold, hold! Lieutenant—sir—Montano—gentle-
     men!
Have you forgot all sense of place and duty?
Hold! The General speaks to you. Hold, hold, for shame! 170

173. **heaven hath forbid the Ottomites**: heaven prevented the Turks' attack by destroying their fleet.

175. **to carve for his own rage**: to carve for oneself meant to indulge one's own fancy.

181-83. **but now . . . but now**: one minute . . . the next minute

182. **In quarter**: behaving properly

184. **some planet had unwitted men**: the influence of a planet had unsettled men's wits.

187. **peevish odds**: silly quarrel

190. **are thus forgot**: have thus forgotten yourself

192. **were wont be**: are accustomed to be

193. **stillness**: synonymous with "gravity"

195. **censure**: judgment, without the modern connotation of adverse opinion

196. **unlace**: disorder, expose to shame

197. **spend your rich opinion**: squander the value of your good repute

201. **something now offends me**: is somewhat painful to me

Oth. Why, how now, ho? From whence ariseth this?
Are we turned Turks, and to ourselves do that
Which heaven hath forbid the Ottomites?
For Christian shame put by this barbarous brawl!
He that stirs next to carve for his own rage   175
Holds his soul light; he dies upon his motion.
Silence that dreadful bell! It frights the isle
From her propriety. What's the matter, masters?
Honest Iago, that looks dead with grieving,
Speak. Who began this? On thy love, I charge thee.   180
    Iago. I do not know. Friends all but now, even now,
In quarter, and in terms like bride and groom
Devesting them for bed; and then, but now
(As if some planet had unwitted men)
Swords out, and tilting one at other's breast   185
In opposition bloody. I cannot speak
Any beginning to this peevish odds,
And would in action glorious I had lost
Those legs that brought me to a part of it!
    Oth. How comes it, Michael, you are thus forgot?   190
    Cas. I pray you pardon me; I cannot speak.
    Oth. Worthy Montano, you were wont be civil;
The gravity and stillness of your youth
The world hath noted, and your name is great
In mouths of wisest censure. What's the matter   195
That you unlace your reputation thus
And spend your rich opinion for the name
Of a night-brawler? Give me answer to't.
    Mon. Worthy Othello, I am hurt to danger.
Your officer, Iago, can inform you,   200
While I spare speech, which something now offends me,
Of all that I do know; nor know I aught

208. **My blood begins my safer guides to rule:** my anger begins to overpower my discretion.

209. **collied:** literally, "blackened with coal"; obscured

212. **sink in my rebuke:** that is, be cut down by my sword

214. **approved in this offense:** proved at fault in the brawl

218. **manage:** engage in; **domestic:** personal

219. **on the court and guard of safety:** while on duty at the headquarters of the watch

221. **partially affined, or leagued in office:** biased by affection or comradeship

232. **To execute upon him:** to exact satisfaction from him, not necessarily to kill him

By me that's said or done amiss this night,
Unless self-charity be sometimes a vice,
And to defend ourselves it be a sin   205
When violence assails us.
   Oth.   Now, by heaven,
My blood begins my safer guides to rule,
And passion, having my best judgment collied,
Assays to lead the way. If I once stir   210
Or do but lift this arm, the best of you
Shall sink in my rebuke. Give me to know
How this foul rout began, who set it on;
And he that is approved in this offense,
Though he had twinned with me, both at a birth,   215
Shall lose me. What! in a town of war,
Yet wild, the people's hearts brimful of fear,
To manage private and domestic quarrel?
In night, and on the court and guard of safety?
'Tis monstrous. Iago, who began 't?   220
   Mon. If partially affined, or leagued in office,
Thou dost deliver more or less than truth,
Thou art no soldier.
   Iago.   Touch me not so near.
I had rather have this tongue cut from my mouth   225
Than it should do offense to Michael Cassio.
Yet I persuade myself, to speak the truth
Shall nothing wrong him. Thus it is, General.
Montano and myself being in speech,
There comes a fellow crying out for help,   230
And Cassio following him with determined sword
To execute upon him. Sir, this gentleman
Steps in to Cassio and entreats his pause.
Myself the crying fellow did pursue,

237-38. the rather/ For that: the sooner because
252. mince: belittle

Lest by his clamor (as it so fell out) 235
The town might fall in fright. He, swift of foot,
Outran my purpose; and I returned the rather
For that I heard the clink and fall of swords,
And Cassio high in oath; which till tonight
I ne'er might say before. When I came back 240
(For this was brief) I found them close together
At blow and thrust, even as again they were
When you yourself did part them.
More of this matter cannot I report;
But men are men; the best sometimes forget. 245
Though Cassio did some little wrong to him,
As men in rage strike those that wish them best,
Yet surely Cassio I believe received
From him that fled some strange indignity,
Which patience could not pass. 250
    Oth.   I know, Iago,
Thy honesty and love doth mince this matter,
Making it light to Cassio. Cassio, I love thee;
But never more be officer of mine.

              Enter *Desdemona, attended.*

Look if my gentle love be not raised up! 255
I'll make thee an example.
    Des.   What's the matter, dear?
    Oth. All's well now, sweeting; come away to bed.
[*To Montano*] Sir, for your hurts, myself will be your sur-
    geon. 260
Lead him off.
                    [*Exit Montano, attended.*]
Iago, look with care about the town
And silence those whom this vile brawl distracted.

275-76. **imposition**: that is, it is imposed on one by others.

280. **more in policy than in malice**: more as an example of discipline than because of personal resentment

281-82. **beat his offenseless dog to affright an imperious lion**: exert authority over a weak object in order to intimidate one more fearsome; that is, Cassio as opposed to the main force of the army

285. **speak parrot**: talk senselessly, as a parrot will repeat words without understanding

286. **fustian**: nonsense

Come, Desdemona. 'Tis the soldiers' life
To have their balmy slumbers waked with strife.   265
                    Exeunt [all but Iago and Cassio].
     Iago. What, are you hurt, Lieutenant?
     Cas. Ay, past all surgery.
     Iago. Marry, God forbid!
     Cas. Reputation, reputation, reputation! O, I have lost
my reputation! I have lost the immortal part of myself,   270
and what remains is bestial. My reputation, Iago, my
reputation!
     Iago. As I am an honest man, I thought you had re-
ceived some bodily wound; there is more sense in that
than in reputation. Reputation is an idle and most false im-   275
position; oft got without merit and lost without deserving.
You have lost no reputation at all unless you repute yourself such a loser. What, man! there are ways to recover
the General again. You are but now cast in his mood—a
punishment more in policy than in malice, even so as one   280
would beat his offenseless dog to affright an imperious
lion. Sue to him again, and he's yours.
     Cas. I will rather sue to be despised than to deceive so
good a commander with so slight, so drunken, and so in-
discreet an officer. Drunk? and speak parrot? and squab-   285
ble? swagger? swear? and discourse fustian with one's
own shadow? O thou invisible spirit of wine, if thou hast
no name to be known by, let us call thee devil!
     Iago. What was he that you followed with your sword?
What had he done to you?   290
     Cas. I know not.
     Iago. Is't possible?
     Cas. I remember a mass of things, but nothing dis-
tinctly; a quarrel, but nothing wherefore. O God, that

296. **pleasance:** merriment

297. **applause:** sociability

302. **frankly:** unreservedly

308. **Hydra:** a multi-headed monster of Greek mythology

310. **presently:** almost immediately after

311. **inordinate:** in excess of moderation

313. **familiar:** friendly, with a pun on "familiar," a benevolent spirit as compared with the devil Cassio says inhabits wine

316. **approved:** confirmed; see II. [iii.] 214.

323. **free:** generous; **apt:** responsive

men should put an enemy in their mouths to steal away 295
their brains! that we should with joy, pleasance, revel,
and applause transform ourselves into beasts!

Iago. Why, but you are now well enough. How came
you thus recovered?

Cas. It hath pleased the devil drunkenness to give 300
place to the devil wrath. One unperfectness shows me another, to make me frankly despise myself.

Iago. Come, you are too severe a moraler. As the time,
the place, and the condition of this country stands, I
could heartily wish this had not so befall'n; but since it is 305
as it is, mend it for your own good.

Cas. I will ask him for my place again: he shall tell me
I am a drunkard! Had I as many mouths as Hydra, such
an answer would stop them all. To be now a sensible
man, by-and-by a fool, and presently a beast! O strange! 310
Every inordinate cup is unblest, and the ingredient is a
devil.

Iago. Come, come, good wine is a good familiar creature if it be well used. Exclaim no more against it. And,
good Lieutenant, I think you think I love you. 315

Cas. I have well approved it, sir. I drunk?

Iago. You or any man living may be drunk at a time,
man. I'll tell you what you shall do. Our General's wife is
now the General. I may say so in this respect, for that he
hath devoted and given up himself to the contemplation, 320
mark, and denotement of her parts and graces. Confess
yourself freely to her. Importune her help to put you in
your place again. She is of so free, so kind, so apt, so
blessed a disposition she holds it a vice in her goodness
not to do more than she is requested. This broken joint 325

326. **splinter:** repair with a splint

327. **lay:** wager

332. **freely:** without qualification

340. **Probal to thinking:** probable, reasonable

342. **inclining:** compliant

349-50. **Even as her appetite shall play the god/ With his weak function:** just as her wishes completely master his weak faculties

352. **Divinity of hell:** that is, the foregoing is hell's own theology.

353. **put on:** urge

354. **suggest:** tempt

356. **Plies:** beseeches

between you and her husband entreat her to splinter; and
my fortunes against any lay worth naming, this crack of
your love shall grow stronger than 'twas before.

Cas. You advise me well.

Iago. I protest, in the sincerity of love and honest 330
kindness.

Cas. I think it freely; and betimes in the morning will
I beseech the virtuous Desdemona to undertake for me.
I am desperate of my fortunes if they check me here.

Iago. You are in the right. Good night, Lieutenant; I 335
must to the watch.

Cas. Good night, honest Iago. *Exit.*

Iago. And what's he then that says I play the villain,
When this advice is free I give and honest,
Probal to thinking, and indeed the course   340
To win the Moor again? For 'tis most easy
Th' inclining Desdemona to subdue
In any honest suit. She's framed as fruitful
As the free elements. And then for her
To win the Moor—were't to renounce his baptism,   345
All seals and symbols of redeemed sin—
His soul is so enfettered to her love
That she may make, unmake, do what she list,
Even as her appetite shall play the god
With his weak function. How am I then a villain   350
To counsel Cassio to this parallel course,
Directly to his good? Divinity of hell!
When devils will the blackest sins put on,
They do suggest at first with heavenly shows,
As I do now. For whiles this honest fool   355
Plies Desdemona to repair his fortune,
And she for him pleads strongly to the Moor,

Hunting with hounds.
From George Turberville, *Noble arte of venerie or hunting* (1576).

359. **repeals**: recalls (to his position)

366-67. **not like a hound that hunts, but one that
fills up the cry**: "for no useful purpose," referring to
the practice of using dogs for the effect of their
voices in the pack rather than to hunt the quarry

379. **fruits that blossom first will first be ripe**:
that is, it is natural that matters will progress in
proper order according to their commencement.

I'll pour this pestilence into his ear—
That she repeals him for her body's lust;
And by how much she strives to do him good,   360
She shall undo her credit with the Moor.
So will I turn her virtue into pitch,
And out of her own goodness make the net
That shall enmesh them all.

Enter *Roderigo*.

                How now, Roderigo?   365
    Rod. I do follow here in the chase, not like a hound
that hunts, but one that fills up the cry. My money is almost spent; I have been tonight exceedingly well
cudgelled; and I think the issue will be, I shall have so
much experience for my pains; and so, with no money at 370
all, and a little more wit, return again to Venice.
    Iago. How poor are they that have not patience!
What wound did ever heal but by degrees?
Thou know'st we work by wit, and not by witchcraft;
And wit depends on dilatory time.   375
Does't not go well? Cassio hath beaten thee,
And thou by that small hurt hast cashiered Cassio.
Though other things grow fair against the sun,
Yet fruits that blossom first will first be ripe.
Content thyself awhile. By th' mass, 'tis morning!   380
Pleasure and action make the hours seem short.
Retire thee; go where thou art billeted.
Away, I say! Thou shalt know more hereafter.
Nay, get thee gone!

                          Exit Roderigo.

386. **move:** intercede
389. **jump:** at the very moment
391. **coldness:** indifference, slowness to act

               Two things are to be done: 385
My wife must move for Cassio to her mistress;
I'll set her on;
Myself a while to draw the Moor apart
And bring him jump when he may Cassio find
Soliciting his wife. Ay, that's the way!   390
Dull not device by coldness and delay.

                              Exit.

THE TRAGEDY OF

OTHELLO,

THE MOOR OF VENICE

ACT III

III. i. Cassio appears before the Castle, where he meets Iago, who sends Emilia to talk with him. She reports that Desdemona is already pleading for him but Cassio wants a private interview with her. All of this, of course, is precisely as Iago has contrived it.

⁖⁖⁖⁖⁖⁖⁖⁖⁖⁖⁖⁖⁖⁖⁖⁖⁖⁖⁖⁖⁖⁖⁖⁖⁖⁖⁖⁖⁖⁖⁖⁖⁖⁖

1. **content your pains:** reward your efforts
2. **bid "Good morrow, General":** it was an English custom to awaken people of consequence by serenades on special occasions, particularly the day after their marriage.
3-4. **have your instruments been at Naples, that they speak i' th' nose thus:** many references occur in Elizabethan literature to the effect of syphilis eating away the nose and to the frequency of contagion in Naples.
12. **of all loves:** for the love you bear him

ACT III

Scene I. [Cyprus. Before the Castle.]

Enter *Cassio,* with *Musicians.*

Cas. Masters, play here, I will content your pains:
Something that's brief; and bid "Good morrow, General."
They play.

Enter the *Clown.*

Clown. Why, masters, have your instruments been at
Naples, that they speak i' th' nose thus?

Mus. How, sir, how? 5

Clown. Are these, I pray, called wind instruments?

Mus. Ay, marry, are they, sir.

Clown. O, thereby hangs a tail.

Mus. Whereby hangs a tale, sir?

Clown. Marry, sir, by many a wind instrument that I 10
know. But, masters, here's money for you; and the General
so likes your music that he desires you, of all loves, to
make no more noise with it.

Mus. Well, sir, we will not.

Clown. If you have any music that may not be heard, 15
to't again. But, as they say, to hear music the General
does not greatly care.

54

A serenade.
From the illustration to an old ballad.

23. **keep up:** keep to yourself; **quillets:** puns

28. **seem to notify unto her:** tell her. The Clown indulges in high-flown speech for comic effect.

30. **In happy time:** in other words, "You're just the man I want to see."

37. **presently:** immediately

38. **mean:** means

42-3. **I never knew/ A Florentine more kind and honest:** that is, he is as kind and honest as one of my fellow citizens.

Mus. We have none such, sir.

Clown. Then put up your pipes in your bag, for I'll
away. Go, vanish into air, away!   20

Exeunt Musicians.

Cas. Dost thou hear, my honest friend?

Clown. No, I hear not your honest friend. I hear you.

Cas. Prithee keep up thy quillets. There's a poor piece
of gold for thee. If the gentlewoman that attends the
General's wife be stirring, tell her there's one Cassio en-   25
treats her a little favor of speech. Wilt thou do this?

Clown. She is stirring, sir. If she will stir hither, I shall
seem to notify unto her.

Cas. Do, good my friend.

Exit Clown.

Enter *Iago.*

In happy time, Iago.   30

Iago. You have not been abed then?

Cas. Why, no. The day had broke
Before we parted. I have made bold, Iago,
To send in to your wife. My suit to her
Is that she will to virtuous Desdemona   35
Procure me some access.

Iago.   I'll send her to you presently;
And I'll devise a mean to draw the Moor
Out of the way, that your converse and business
May be more free.   40

Cas. I humbly thank you for't.

Exit [Iago].

I never knew
A Florentine more kind and honest.

45. **your displeasure:** your loss of favor

48-9. **of . . . great affinity:** strong in family alliances; **in wholesome wisdom:** for discretion's sake

50. **might:** could

52. **front:** forelock. A proverb from classical literature cautioned that opportunity should be seized by the forelock because it was bald behind. Time and Fortune were both pictured accordingly.

53. **bring you in:** reinstate you

57. **Desdemon:** this variant form of Desdemona is used several times in the Folio where the final vowel would sound awkward.

59. **bestow:** accommodate

IIIIIIIIIIIIIIIIIIIIIIIIIIIIIIIIIIIIIIIIIIIIIIIIIIIIIIIIIIIIIII

III. ii.

3. **works:** fortified walls

Military tactics of the sixteenth century.
From Olaus Magnus, *Historia de gentibus* (1555).

Enter *Emilia.*

Emil. Good morrow, good Lieutenant. I am sorry
For your displeasure; but all will sure be well.   45
The General and his wife are talking of it.
And she speaks for you stoutly. The Moor replies
That he you hurt is of great fame in Cyprus
And great affinity, and that in wholesome wisdom
He might not but refuse you. But he protests he loves you,   50
And needs no other suitor but his likings
To take the safest occasion by the front
To bring you in again.
    Cas.   Yet I beseech you,
If you think fit, or that it may be done,   55
Give me advantage of some brief discourse
With Desdemon alone.
    Emil.   Pray you come in.
I will bestow you where you shall have time
To speak your bosom freely.   60
    Cas.   I am much bound to you.
                                Exeunt.

Scene II. [Cyprus. Within the Castle.]

Enter *Othello, Iago,* and *Gentlemen.*

Oth. These letters give, Iago, to the pilot
And by him do my duties to the senate.
That done, I will be walking on the works.
Repair there to me.

III. iii. Iago's success in arousing Othello's jealousy begins to appear. Othello observes Cassio leaving Desdemona, who immediately begins to urge him to recall Cassio. When Othello has dismissed his wife, Iago insinuates that the meeting is suspicious, that Cassio may not be as honest as he seems, and that he, Iago, knows more than he is telling. He succeeds in making Othello doubtful of his wife's love and loyalty.

Emilia delivers to Iago a handkerchief that Othello has given Desdemona, and Iago drops it where Cassio will find it. Adroitly Iago fills Othello's mind with suspicion of Desdemona until Othello is convinced, but nevertheless demands proof. Iago describes overhearing Cassio mutter in his sleep of Desdemona and their love and asserts that he has seen him wipe his beard with her handkerchief. Othello swears vengeance on both of them, and Iago promises to see that Cassio is killed.

          ▭▭▭▭▭▭▭▭▭▭▭▭▭▭▭▭▭

14-5. in strangeness stand no farther off/ Than in a politic distance: be no more aloof than policy makes necessary

18. feed upon such nice and waterish diet: be stimulated by such minute and trifling considerations

19. breed itself so out of circumstance: be so perpetuated by new happenings

Iago.   Well, my good lord, I'll do't.   5
Oth. This fortification, gentlemen, shall we see't?
Gent. We'll wait upon your lordship.

                                    Exeunt.

Scene III. [Cyprus. The garden of the Castle.]

Enter *Desdemona, Cassio,* and *Emilia.*

Des. Be thou assured, good Cassio, I will do
All my abilities in thy behalf.
    Emil. Good madam, do. I warrant it grieves my hus-
        band
As if the cause were his.   5
    Des. O, that's an honest fellow. Do not doubt, Cassio,
But I will have my lord and you again
As friendly as you were.
    Cas.   Bounteous madam,
Whatever shall become of Michael Cassio,   10
He's never anything but your true servant.
    Des. I know't; I thank you. You do love my lord;
You have known him long; and be you well assured
He shall in strangeness stand no farther off
Than in a politic distance.   15
    Cas.   Ay, but, lady,
That policy may either last so long,
Or feed upon such nice and waterish diet,
Or breed itself so out of circumstance,
That, I being absent, and my place supplied,   20
My general will forget my love and service.

26. **watch him tame:** subdue him by keeping him awake, a device used in taming hawks

27. **shrift:** confessional, where his faults are evaluated

31. **give thy cause away:** give up your cause

Des. Do not doubt that. Before Emilia here
I give thee warrant of thy place. Assure thee,
If I do vow a friendship, I'll perform it
To the last article. My lord shall never rest;   25
I'll watch him tame and talk him out of patience;
His bed shall seem a school, his board a shrift;
I'll intermingle everything he does
With Cassio's suit. Therefore be merry, Cassio,
For thy solicitor shall rather die   30
Than give thy cause away.

Enter *Othello* and *Iago*.

Emil. Madam, here comes my lord.
Cas. Madam, I'll take my leave.
Des. Why, stay, and hear me speak.
Cas. Madam, not now. I am very ill at ease,   35
Unfit for mine own purposes.
Des. Well, do your discretion.

                                        Exit Cassio.

Iago. Ha! I like not that.
Oth.   What dost thou say?
Iago. Nothing, my lord; or if—I know not what.   40
Oth. Was not that Cassio parted from my wife?
Iago. Cassio, my lord? No, sure, I cannot think it,
That he would steal away so guilty-like,
Seeing you coming.
Oth.   I do believe 'twas he.   45
Des. How now, my lord?
I have been talking with a suitor here,
A man that languishes in your displeasure.
Oth. Who is't you mean?

52. **reconciliation:** submission; that is, "accept his sincere repentance and forgive him."

73. **in our common reason:** considered as we commonly look at such things

74-5. **the wars must make examples/ Out of their best:** military discipline requires that the best men serve as examples to the army as a whole.

75-6. **not almost a fault/ T' incur a private check:** hardly enough of a fault to merit even a private rebuke

79. **stand so mamm'ring on:** remain in such hesitation about

Des. Why, your lieutenant, Cassio. Good my lord,   50
If I have any grace or power to move you,
His present reconciliation take;
For if he be not one that truly loves you,
That errs in ignorance, and not in cunning,
I have no judgment in an honest face.   55
I prithee call him back.
   Oth.   Went he hence now?
   Des. Yes, faith; so humbled
That he hath left part of his grief with me
To suffer with him. Good love, call him back.   60
   Oth. Not now, sweet Desdemon; some other time.
   Des. But shall't be shortly?
   Oth.   The sooner, sweet, for you.
   Des. Shall't be tonight at supper?
   Oth.   No, not tonight.   65
   Des. Tomorrow dinner then?
   Oth.   I shall not dine at home.
I meet the captains at the citadel.
   Des. Why then, tomorrow night, or Tuesday morn,
Or Tuesday noon or night, or Wednesday morn.   70
I prithee name the time, but let it not
Exceed three days. I' faith, he's penitent;
And yet his trespass, in our common reason
(Save that, they say, the wars must make examples
Out of their best) is not almost a fault   75
T' incur a private check. When shall he come?
Tell me, Othello. I wonder in my soul
What you could ask me that I should deny
Or stand so mamm'ring on. What? Michael Cassio,
That came a-wooing with you, and so many a time,   80
When I have spoke of you dispraisingly,

92. **poise:** weight in the scales

93. **fearful:** requiring serious thought of the consequences

102. **wretch:** a term of endearment

Hath ta'en your part—to have so much to do
To bring him in? Trust me, I could do much—
   Oth. Prithee no more. Let him come when he will!
I will deny thee nothing.   85
   Des.   Why, this is not a boon;
'Tis as I should entreat you wear your gloves,
Or feed on nourishing dishes, or keep you warm,
Or sue to you to do a peculiar profit
To your own person. Nay, when I have a suit   90
Wherein I mean to touch your love indeed,
It shall be full of poise and difficult weight,
And fearful to be granted.
   Oth.   I will deny thee nothing!
Whereon I do beseech thee grant me this,   95
To leave me but a little to myself.
   Des. Shall I deny you? No. Farewell, my lord.
   Oth. Farewell, my Desdemon. I'll come to thee
     straight.
   Des. Emilia, come.—Be as your fancies teach you.   100
Whate'er you be, I am obedient.
               Exeunt Desdemona and Emilia.
   Oth. Excellent wretch! Perdition catch my soul
But I do love thee! and when I love thee not,
Chaos is come again.
   Iago. My noble lord—   105
   Oth.   What dost thou say, Iago?
   Iago. Did Michael Cassio, when you wooed my lady,
Know of your love?
   Oth. He did, from first to last. Why dost thou ask?
   Iago. But for a satisfaction of my thought;   110
No further harm.
   Oth.   Why of thy thought, Iago?

134. **conceit:** imagining
140. **stops:** hesitations
142. **tricks of custom:** habitual tricks
143. **close dilations:** trustworthy signs of emotion

Iago. I did not think he had been acquainted with her.
Oth. O, yes, and went between us very oft.
Iago. Indeed?   115
Oth. Indeed? Ay, indeed! Discern'st thou aught in
    that?
Is he not honest?
Iago.   Honest, my lord?
Oth.   Honest? Ay, honest.   120
Iago. My lord, for aught I know.
Oth. What dost thou think?
Iago.   Think, my lord?
Oth.   Think, my lord?
By heaven, he echoes me,   125
As if there were some monster in his thought
Too hideous to be shown. Thou dost mean something.
I heard thee say even now, thou lik'st not that,
When Cassio left my wife. What didst not like?
And when I told thee he was of my counsel   130
In my whole course of wooing, thou cried'st "Indeed?"
And didst contract and purse thy brow together,
As if thou then hadst shut up in thy brain
Some horrible conceit. If thou dost love me,
Show me thy thought.   135
Iago. My lord, you know I love you.
Oth.   I think thou dost;
And, for I know thou'rt full of love and honesty
And weigh'st thy words before thou giv'st them breath,
Therefore these stops of thine fright me the more;   140
For such things in a false disloyal knave
Are tricks of custom; but in a man that's just
They are close dilations, working from the heart
That passion cannot rule.

149. **seem none:** that is, not seem to be men at all

158. **I am not bound to that all slaves are free to:** I am not obliged to express my inmost thoughts, which even slaves are free to reserve.

163. **leets:** synonymous with **law days;** that is, regular court sessions

169. **Though I perchance am vicious in my guess:** since I may be wrong in my suspicion

171. **jealousy:** suspiciousness

173. **conceits:** imagines; see III. iii. 134.

175. **scattering:** random

176. **It were not for:** it would not accord with

Iago.   For Michael Cassio,   145
I dare be sworn I think that he is honest.
   Oth. I think so too.
   Iago.   Men should be what they seem;
Or those that be not, would they might seem none!
   Oth. Certain, men should be what they seem.   150
   Iago. Why then, I think Cassio's an honest man.
   Oth. Nay, yet there's more in this.
I prithee speak to me, as to thy thinkings,
As thou dost ruminate, and give thy worst of thoughts
The worst of words.   155
   Iago.   Good my lord, pardon me.
Though I am bound to every act of duty,
I am not bound to that all slaves are free to.
Utter my thoughts? Why, say they are vile and false,
As where's that palace whereinto foul things   160
Sometimes intrude not? Who has a breast so pure
But some uncleanly apprehensions
Keep leets and law days, and in session sit
With meditations lawful?
   Oth. Thou dost conspire against thy friend, Iago,   165
If thou but think'st him wronged, and mak'st his ear
A stranger to thy thoughts.
   Iago.   I do beseech you—
Though I perchance am vicious in my guess
(As I confess it is my nature's plague   170
To spy into abuses, and oft my jealousy
Shapes faults that are not)—that your wisdom
From one that so imperfectly conceits
Would take no notice, nor build yourself a trouble
Out of his scattering and unsure observance.   175
It were not for your quiet nor your good,

181. **immediate:** nearest, in the sense of being most important

192. **mock:** toy with in the manner of a cat with a mouse

199. **fineless:** limitless

207. **resolved:** satisfied as to the truth

Nor for my manhood, honesty, or wisdom,
To let you know my thoughts.
    Oth.   What dost thou mean?
    Iago. Good name in man and woman, dear my lord,   180
Is the immediate jewel of their souls.
Who steals my purse steals trash; 'tis something, nothing;
'Twas mine, 'tis his, and has been slave to thousands;
But he that filches from me my good name
Robs me of that which not enriches him   185
And makes me poor indeed.
    Oth. By heaven, I'll know thy thoughts!
    Iago. You cannot, if my heart were in your hand;
Nor shall not whilst 'tis in my custody.
    Oth. Ha!   190
    Iago.   O, beware, my lord, of jealousy!
It is the green-eyed monster, which doth mock
The meat it feeds on. That cuckold lives in bliss
Who, certain of his fate, loves not his wronger;
But O, what damned minutes tells he o'er   195
Who dotes, yet doubts; suspects, yet strongly loves!
    Oth. O misery!
    Iago. Poor and content is rich, and rich enough;
But riches fineless is as poor as winter
To him that ever fears he shall be poor.   200
Good heaven, the souls of all my tribe defend
From jealousy!
    Oth.   Why, why is this?
Think'st thou I'd make a life of jealousy,
To follow still the changes of the moon   205
With fresh suspicions? No! To be once in doubt
Is once to be resolved. Exchange me for a goat
When I shall turn the business of my soul

209. **exsufflicate:** found nowhere except in this passage. Presumably Shakespeare formed the word from *exsufflare*, "to contemn, despise," and the meaning is "odious, contemptible"; **blown** means literally "fly-blown" and is therefore synonymous.

213. **Where virtue is, these are more virtuous:** these excellent characteristics are all the more admirable in a virtuous person.

214. **weak merits:** small claim to good looks

215. **revolt:** infidelity

225. **not jealous nor secure:** neither suspicious nor overly trustful

227. **self-bounty:** natural charity

237. **go to then:** "There you are!"

239. **seel:** seal; see I. iii. 291; **oak:** that is, the grain of oak

To such exsufflicate and blown surmises,
Matching thy inference. 'Tis not to make me jealous   210
To say my wife is fair, feeds well, loves company,
Is free of speech, sings, plays, and dances well.
Where virtue is, these are more virtuous.
Nor from mine own weak merits will I draw
The smallest fear or doubt of her revolt,   215
For she had eyes, and chose me. No, Iago;
I'll see before I doubt; when I doubt, prove;
And on the proof there is no more but this—
Away at once with love or jealousy!

   Iago. I am glad of it; for now I shall have reason   220
To show the love and duty that I bear you
With franker spirit. Therefore, as I am bound,
Receive it from me. I speak not yet of proof.
Look to your wife; observe her well with Cassio;
Wear your eye thus, not jealous nor secure.   225
I would not have your free and noble nature,
Out of self-bounty, be abused. Look to't.
I know our country disposition well:
In Venice they do let heaven see the pranks
They dare not show their husbands; their best conscience   230
Is not to leave't undone, but keep't unknown.

   Oth. Dost thou say so?

   Iago. She did deceive her father, marrying you;
And when she seemed to shake and fear your looks,
She loved them most.   235

   Oth.   And so she did.

   Iago.   Why, go to then!
She that, so young, could give out such a seeming
To seel her father's eyes up close as oak—

240. **I am much to blame:** I deserve censure.

250. **grosser:** greater

254. **success:** consequence

258. **honest:** physically faithful

262. **affect:** incline to

263. **complexion:** nature, temperament

265. **will:** sexual appetite; see I. iii. 369.

266. **disproportion:** abnormality

267. **in position:** in expounding this theory

269-70. **Her will, recoiling to her better judgment,/ May fall to match you with her country forms:** her appetite, overcome by her better judgment, may compare you with men of her own race.

271. **happily:** perhaps, haply

He thought 'twas witchcraft—but I am much to blame. 240
I humbly do beseech you of your pardon
For too much loving you.
    Oth.   I am bound to thee for ever.
    Iago. I see this hath a little dashed your spirits.
    Oth. Not a jot, not a jot. 245
    Iago.   I' faith, I fear it has.
I hope you will consider what is spoke
Comes from my love. But I do see y'are moved.
I am to pray you not to strain my speech
To grosser issues nor to larger reach 250
Than to suspicion.
    Oth. I will not.
    Iago.   Should you do so, my lord,
My speech should fall into such vile success
As my thoughts aim not at. Cassio's my worthy friend— 255
My lord, I see y'are moved.
    Oth.   No, not much moved.
I do not think but Desdemona's honest.
    Iago. Long live she so! and long live you to think so!
    Oth. And yet, how nature erring from itself— 260
    Iago. Ay, there's the point! as (to be bold with you)
Not to affect many proposed matches
Of her own clime, complexion, and degree,
Whereto we see in all things nature tends—
Foh! one may smell in such a will most rank, 265
Foul disproportion, thoughts unnatural—
But pardon me—I do not in position
Distinctly speak of her; though I may fear
Her will, recoiling to her better judgment,
May fall to match you with her country forms, 270
And happily repent.

284. **means:** that is, means of suing to you

285. **strain his entertainment:** urge his reappointment. "Entertain" had the meaning "hire" or "take on as a retainer."

290. **free:** innocent

291. **government:** self-control

295. **haggard:** faithless. A haggard is a hawk which has not been tamed.

296. **jesses:** straps of leather by which a hawk was tethered to a leash

297. **whistle her off:** dismiss her. A whistle was the hawker's signal of dismissal when releasing his hawk; **down the wind:** a hawk properly was flown against wind, and "down the wind" became a proverbial phrase to signify a desperate state of luck.

299. **parts:** qualities; **conversation:** general address, not merely "talk"

300. **chamberers:** wanton persons

A haggard falcon
From Simon Latham, *Lathams Falconry, or The Faulcons Lure, and Cure* (1633).

66

   Oth.   Farewell, farewell!
If more thou dost perceive, let me know more.
Set on thy wife to observe. Leave me, Iago.
   Iago. My lord, I take my leave.   [*Walks away.*] 275
   Oth. Why did I marry? This honest creature doubtless
Sees and knows more, much more, than he unfolds.
   Iago. [*Returns*] My lord, I would I might entreat your
     Honor
To scan this thing no further. Leave it to time.   280
Although 'tis fit that Cassio have his place,
For sure he fills it up with great ability,
Yet, if you please to hold him off awhile,
You shall by that perceive him and his means.
Note if your lady strain his entertainment   285
With any strong or vehement importunity.
Much will be seen in that. In the mean time
Let me be thought too busy in my fears
(As worthy cause I have to fear I am)
And hold her free, I do beseech your Honor.   290
   Oth. Fear not my government.
   Iago. I once more take my leave.   *Exit.*
   Oth. This fellow's of exceeding honesty,
And knows all qualities, with a learned spirit
Of human dealings. If I do prove her haggard,   295
Though that her jesses were my dear heartstrings,
I'd whistle her off and let her down the wind
To prey at fortune. Haply, for I am black
And have not those soft parts of conversation
That chamberers have, or for I am declined   300
Into the vale of years (yet that's not much),
She's gone. I am abused, and my relief
Must be to loathe her. O curse of marriage,

308. **great ones:** those of high station

309. **Prerogatived are they less:** they are less exempt

311. **forked plague:** a reference to the proverbial horns of the cuckold

312. **When we do quicken:** when life first stirs in us

313. **heaven mocks itself:** that is, by creating a woman with only the appearance of divine purity

316. **generous:** illustrious, those of high position

322. **watching:** wakefulness

325. **napkin:** handkerchief

That we can call these delicate creatures ours,
And not their appetites! I had rather be a toad   305
And live upon the vapor of a dungeon
Than keep a corner in the thing I love
For others' uses. Yet 'tis the plague of great ones;
Prerogatived are they less than the base.
'Tis destiny unshunnable, like death: 310
Even then this forked plague is fated to us
When we do quicken. Desdemona comes.

          Enter Desdemona and Emilia.

If she be false, O, then heaven mocks itself!
I'll not believe't.
     Des.   How now, my dear Othello?   315
Your dinner, and the generous islanders
By you invited, do attend your presence.
     Oth. I am to blame.
     Des.   Why do you speak so faintly?
Are you not well?   320
     Oth. I have a pain upon my forehead, here.
     Des. Faith, that's with watching; 'twill away again.
Let me but bind it hard, within this hour
It will be well.
     Oth.   Your napkin is too little.   325
               [*He pushes it away and it drops.*]
Let it alone. Come, I'll go in with you.
     Des. I am very sorry that you are not well.
                    Exeunt Othello and Desdemona.
     Emil. I am glad I have found this napkin.
This was her first remembrance from the Moor.

334. **have the work ta'en out:** have the embroidered design copied

351. **to th' advantage:** advantageously

My wayward husband hath a hundred times   330
Wooed me to steal it; but she so loves the token
(For he conjured her she should ever keep it)
That she reserves it evermore about her
To kiss and talk to. I'll have the work ta'en out
And give't Iago.   335
What he will do with it heaven knows, not I;
I nothing but to please his fantasy.

                    Enter *Iago*.

   Iago. How now? What do you here alone?
   Emil. Do not you chide; I have a thing for you.
   Iago. A thing for me? It is a common thing—   340
   Emil. Ha?
   Iago. To have a foolish wife.
   Emil. O, is that all? What will you give me now
For that same handkerchief?
   Iago.   What handkerchief?   345
   Emil. What handkerchief?
Why, that the Moor first gave to Desdemona;
That which so often you did bid me steal.
   Iago. Hast stol'n it from her?
   Emil. No, faith; she let it drop by negligence,   350
And to th' advantage, I, being here, took't up.
Look, here it is.
   Iago.   A good wench! Give it me.
   Emil. What will you do with't, that you have been so
      earnest   355
To have me filch it?
   Iago.   Why, what's that to you?
                                        [*Snatches it.*]

360. **lack:** miss

361. **Be not you acknown on't:** act as though you knew nothing of it.

369. **distaste:** taste unpleasant

370. **with a little act:** after brief action

371. **mines of sulphur:** sulphur mines of the Æolian Islands

373. **mandragora:** the plant *Mandragora officinarum,* used to induce healing sleep

376. **ow'dst:** possessed

385. **free:** that is, free of care

MANDRAGORAS.

FOEMINE   MARIS

Mandragora officinarum.
From Rembert Dodoens, *Purgantium aliarumque* (1574).

69

Emil. If it be not for some purpose of import,
Give't me again. Poor lady, she'll run mad
When she shall lack it.   360
    Iago. Be not you acknown on't; I have use for it.
Go, leave me.

                                           Exit Emilia.

I will in Cassio's lodging lose this napkin
And let him find it. Trifles light as air
Are to the jealous confirmations strong   365
As proofs of holy writ. This may do something.
The Moor already changes with my poison.
Dangerous conceits are in their natures poisons
Which at the first are scarce found to distaste,
But with a little act upon the blood   370
Burn like the mines of sulphur. ⟶

                    Enter *Othello.*

                        I did say so.
Look where he comes! Not poppy nor mandragora,
Nor all the drowsy syrups of the world,
Shall ever medicine thee to that sweet sleep   375
Which thou ow'dst yesterday.
    Oth.   Ha! ha! false to me?
    Iago. Why, how now, General? No more of that!
    Oth. Avaunt! be gone! Thou hast set me on the rack.
I swear 'tis better to be much abused   380
Than but to know't a little.
    Iago.   How now, my lord?
    Oth. What sense had I of her stol'n hours of lust?
I saw't not, thought it not, it harmed not me.
I slept the next night well, was free and merry;   385

"Engines" of war.
From Olaus Magnus, *Historia de gentibus* (1555).

387. **wanting:** missing

391. **Pioners:** pioneers, the lowest class of soldiers, who dug trenches, laid mines, etc.

399. **circumstance:** pageantry

400. **mortal:** deadly; see II. i. 80; **engines:** machines, referring here to cannon

411. **probation:** proof

I found not Cassio's kisses on her lips.
He that is robbed, not wanting what is stol'n,
Let him not know't, and he's not robbed at all.
  Iago. I am sorry to hear this.
  Oth. I had been happy if the general camp,   390
Pioners and all, had tasted her sweet body,
So I had nothing known. O, now for ever
Farewell the tranquil mind! farewell content!
Farewell the plumed troop, and the big wars
That make ambition virtue! O, farewell!   395
Farewell the neighing steed and the shrill trump,
The spirit-stirring drum, th' ear-piercing fife,
The royal banner, and all quality,
Pride, pomp, and circumstance of glorious war!
And O ye mortal engines whose rude throats   400
Th' immortal Jove's dread clamors counterfeit,
Farewell! Othello's occupation's gone!
  Iago. Is't possible, my lord?
  Oth. Villain, be sure thou prove my love a whore!
Be sure of it; give me the ocular proof;   405
Or, by the worth of man's eternal soul,
Thou hadst been better have been born a dog
Than answer my waked wrath!
  Iago.   Is't come to this?
  Oth. Make me to see't; or at the least so prove it   410
That the probation bear no hinge nor loop
To hang a doubt on—or woe upon thy life!
  Iago. My noble lord—
  Oth. If thou dost slander her and torture me,
Never pray more; abandon all remorse;   415
On horror's head horrors accumulate;

417. **amazed:** struck dumb with horror

427. **sith:** since

428. **shouldst:** must (in accordance with your appearance of honesty)

430. **that it works for:** that is, the confidence that honesty should inspire

436-38. **If there be cords, or knives,/ Poison, or fire, or suffocating streams,/ I'll not endure it:** in other words, "so long as there are methods of suicide, I will not live thus tortured by doubt."

Do deeds to make heaven weep, all earth amazed;
For nothing canst thou to damnation add
Greater than that.

  Iago.   O grace! O heaven forgive me! 420
Are you a man? Have you a soul or sense?—
God b' wi' you! take mine office. O wretched fool,
That liv'st to make thine honesty a vice!
O monstrous world! Take note, take note, O world,
To be direct and honest is not safe. 425
I thank you for this profit; and from hence
I'll love no friend, sith love breeds such offense.

  Oth. Nay, stay. Thou shouldst be honest.

  Iago. I should be wise; for honesty's a fool
And loses that it works for. 430

  Oth.   By the world,
I think my wife be honest, and think she is not;
I think that thou art just, and think thou art not.
I'll have some proof. Her name, that was as fresh
As Dian's visage, is now begrimed and black 435
As mine own face. If there be cords, or knives,
Poison, or fire, or suffocating streams,
I'll not endure it. Would I were satisfied!

  Iago. I see, sir, you are eaten up with passion.
I do repent me that I put it to you. 440
You would be satisfied?

  Oth.   Would? Nay, I will.

  Iago. And may. But how? how satisfied, my lord?
Would you, the supervisor, grossly gape on?
Behold her topped? 445

  Oth.   Death and damnation! O!

  Iago. It were a tedious difficulty, I think,
To bring them to that prospect. Damn them then,

454. **pride:** heat

456. **strong circumstances:** weighty circumstantial evidence

459. **living reason:** undeniable proof (rather than mere suspicion based on logic)

479. **a foregone conclusion:** a previous actual occurrence

480. **shrewd doubt:** emphatically suspicious circumstance

If ever mortal eyes do see them bolster
More than their own! What then? How then?   450
What shall I say? Where's satisfaction?
It is impossible you should see this,
Were they as prime as goats, as hot as monkeys,
As salt as wolves in pride, and fools as gross
As ignorance made drunk. But yet, I say,   455
If imputation and strong circumstances
Which lead directly to the door of truth
Will give you satisfaction, you may have't.
   Oth. Give me a living reason she's disloyal.
   Iago. I do not like the office.   460
But sith I am entered in this cause so far,
Pricked to't by foolish honesty and love,
I will go on. I lay with Cassio lately,
And being troubled with a raging tooth,
I could not sleep.   465
There are a kind of men so loose of soul
That in their sleeps will mutter their affairs.
One of this kind is Cassio.
In sleep I heard him say, "Sweet Desdemona,
Let us be wary, let us hide our loves!"   470
And then, sir, would he gripe and wring my hand,
Cry "O sweet creature!" and then kiss me hard,
As if he plucked up kisses by the roots
That grew upon my lips; then laid his leg
Over my thigh, and sighed, and kissed, and then   475
Cried "Cursed fate that gave thee to the Moor!"
   Oth. O monstrous! monstrous!
   Iago.   Nay, this was but his dream.
   Oth. But this denoted a foregone conclusion.
'Tis a shrewd doubt, though it be but a dream.   480

487. **wive's:** common Elizabethan usage for "wife's"

502. **fraught:** burden

503. **aspics':** asps'; the asp is a common type of European viper.

504. **Yet be content:** despite everything, control yourself.

507. **Pontic sea:** Black Sea

510. **the Propontic:** the Sea of Marmora; **the Hellespont:** the Bosporus

Iago. And this may help to thicken other proofs
That do demonstrate thinly.

Oth.   I'll tear her all to pieces!

Iago. Nay, but be wise. Yet we see nothing done;
She may be honest yet. Tell me but this—   485
Have you not sometimes seen a handkerchief
Spotted with strawberries in your wive's hand?

Oth. I gave her such a one; 'twas my first gift.

Iago. I know not that; but such a handkerchief
(I am sure it was your wive's) did I today   490
See Cassio wipe his beard with.

Oth.   If't be that—

Iago. If it be that, or any that was hers,
It speaks against her, with the other proofs.

Oth. O, that the slave had forty thousand lives!   495
One is too poor, too weak for my revenge.
Now do I see 'tis true. Look here, Iago:
All my fond love thus do I blow to heaven.
'Tis gone.
Arise, black vengeance, from the hollow hell!   500
Yield up, O love, thy crown and hearted throne
To tyrannous hate! Swell, bosom, with thy fraught,
For 'tis of aspics' tongues!

Iago.   Yet be content.

Oth. O, blood, blood, blood!   505

Iago. Patience, I say. Your mind perhaps may change.

Oth. Never, Iago. Like to the Pontic sea,
Whose icy current and compulsive course
Ne'er feels retiring ebb, but keeps due on
To the Propontic and the Hellespont;   510
Even so my bloody thoughts, with violent pace,
Shall ne'er look back, ne'er ebb to humble love,

514-15. **marble heaven:** "marbled" was in frequent use as an adjective to describe the sky. Streaks of cloud may have prompted Othello to use it here.

517. **engage:** pledge

520. **clip:** embrace

522. **execution:** performance

524-25. **to obey shall be in me remorse,/ What bloody business ever:** I shall obey out of compassion no matter how bloody the action commanded.

526. **greet:** match

Till that a capable and wide revenge
Swallow them up. (*He kneels.*) Now, by yond marble
  heaven,   515
In the due reverence of a sacred vow
I here engage my words.
 Iago.   Do not rise yet.

           Iago kneels.

Witness, you ever-burning lights above,
You elements that clip us round about,   520
Witness that here Iago doth give up
The execution of his wit, hands, heart
To wronged Othello's service! Let him command,
And to obey shall be in me remorse,
What bloody business ever.   525

           [*They rise.*]

 Oth.   I greet thy love,
Not with vain thanks but with acceptance bounteous,
And will upon the instant put thee to't.
Within these three days let me hear thee say
That Cassio's not alive.   530
 Iago. My friend is dead; 'tis done at your request.
But let her live.
 Oth.   Damn her, lewd minx! O, damn her!
Come, go with me apart. I will withdraw
To furnish me with some swift means of death   535
For the fair devil. Now art thou my lieutenant.
 Iago. I am your own for ever.

          Exeunt.

III. iv. Desdemona is still innocently trying to aid Cassio when Othello demands the handkerchief which Iago has "planted" in Cassio's possession. Desdemona denies that it is lost and Othello leaves her angrily as Cassio and Iago approach. Cassio is visited by his mistress, Bianca, to whom he gives the handkerchief, asking her to copy the embroidery for him.

⑅⑅⑅⑅⑅⑅⑅⑅⑅⑅⑅⑅⑅⑅⑅⑅⑅⑅⑅⑅⑅⑅

5-6. **for one to say a soldier lies is stabbing:** that is, soldiers are quick to respond with their daggers when told they lie.

14. **edified:** instructed

25. **crusadoes:** Portuguese gold coins bearing the design of a cross; **but:** but that

Scene IV. [Cyprus. Before the Castle.]

Enter *Desdemona, Emilia,* and *Clown.*

Des. Do you know, sirrah, where Lieutenant Cassio lies?

Clown. I dare not say he lies anywhere.

Des. Why man?

Clown. He's a soldier; and for one to say a soldier lies   5
is stabbing.

Des. Go to. Where lodges he?

Clown. To tell you where he lodges is to tell you where
I lie.

Des. Can anything be made of this?   10

Clown. I know not where he lodges; and for me to
devise a lodging, and say he lies here or he lies there,
were to lie in mine own throat.

Des. Can you enquire him out, and be edified by report?   15

Clown. I will catechize the world for him; that is,
make questions, and by them answer.

Des. Seek him, bid him come hither. Tell him I have
moved my lord on his behalf and hope all will be well.

Clown. To do this is within the compass of man's wit,   20
and therefore I'll attempt the doing it.   *Exit.*

Des. Where should I lose that handkerchief, Emilia?

Emil. I know not, madam.

Des. Believe me, I had rather have lost my purse
Full of crusadoes; and but my noble Moor   25
Is true of mind, and made of no such baseness
As jealous creatures are, it were enough
To put him to ill thinking.

41-2. **liberal . . . hot, and moist:** Othello is debating the possibility of licentiousness in Desdemona's nature as indicated by her hand, though she is unaware of the double meaning of his words.

43. **sequester:** withdrawal

44. **castigation:** mortification of the spirit

51. **our new heraldry is hands, not hearts:** nowadays marriage can be symbolized by the giving of hands, since the heart is not necessarily given too.

55. **salt and sorry rheum:** miserable head cold

Emil.   Is he not jealous?

Des. Who? he? I think the sun where he was born   30
Drew all such humors from him.

Enter *Othello*.

Emil.   Look where he comes.

Des. I will not leave him now till Cassio
Be called to him.—How is't with you, my lord?

Oth. Well, my good lady. [*Aside*] O, hardness to dis-   35
semble!—

How do you, Desdemona?

Des.   Well, my good lord.

Oth. Give me your hand. This hand is moist, my lady.

Des. It yet hath felt no age nor known no sorrow.   40

Oth. This argues fruitfulness and liberal heart.
Hot, hot, and moist. This hand of yours requires
A sequester from liberty, fasting and prayer,
Much castigation, exercise devout;
For here's a young and sweating devil here   45
That commonly rebels. 'Tis a good hand,
A frank one.

Des.   You may, indeed, say so;
For 'twas that hand that gave away my heart.

Oth. A liberal hand! The hearts of old gave hands;   50
But our new heraldry is hands, not hearts.

Des. I cannot speak of this. Come now, your promise!

Oth. What promise, chuck?

Des. I have sent to bid Cassio come speak with you.

Oth. I have a salt and sorry rheum offends me.   55
Lend me thy handkerchief.

Des.   Here, my lord.

67. **amiable:** lovable

75. **such perdition:** such a loss

79-80. **that had numb'red in the world/ The sun to course two hundred compasses:** that was old enough to have counted 200 annual circuits of the sun

83. **mummy:** a term applied to a remedy of supposed magical power consisting of the liquid from an embalmed corpse, pieces of a fresh corpse chemically treated, or the resultant liquid from such a corpse

84. **Conserved:** preserved

Oth. That which I gave you.
Des.   I have it not about me.
Oth. Not?   60
Des.   No indeed, my lord.
Oth.   That is a fault.
That handkerchief
Did an Egyptian to my mother give.
She was a charmer, and could almost read   65
The thoughts of people. She told her, while she kept it,
'Twould make her amiable and subdue my father
Entirely to her love; but if she lost it
Or made a gift of it, my father's eye
Should hold her loathed, and his spirits should hunt 70
After new fancies. She, dying, gave it me,
And bid me, when my fate would have me wive,
To give it her. I did so; and take heed on't;
Make it a darling like your precious eye.
To lose't or give't away were such perdition   75
As nothing else could match.
Des.   Is't possible?
Oth. 'Tis true. There's magic in the web of it.
A sibyl that had numb'red in the world
The sun to course two hundred compasses,   80
In her prophetic fury sewed the work;
The worms were hallowed that did breed the silk;
And it was dyed in mummy which the skilful
Conserved of maidens' hearts.
Des.   I' faith? Is't true?   85
Oth. Most veritable. Therefore look to't well.
Des. Then would to God that I had never seen't!
Oth. Ha! Wherefore?

89. **startingly**: abruptly

102. **sufficient**: capable

110. **you are to blame**: you have no cause to behave so.

118. **hungerly**: hungrily

Des. Why do you speak so startingly and rash?
Oth. Is't lost? Is't gone? Speak, is it out o' th' way? 90
Des. Heaven bless us!
Oth. Say you?
Des. It is not lost. But what an if it were?
Oth. How?
Des. I say it is not lost. 95
Oth.   Fetch't, let me see't!
Des. Why, so I can, sir; but I will not now.
This is a trick to put me from my suit.
Pray you let Cassio be received again.
Oth. Fetch me the handkerchief! My mind misgives. 100
Des. Come, come!
You'll never meet a more sufficient man.
Oth. The handkerchief!
Des.   I pray talk me of Cassio.
Oth. The handkerchief! 105
Des.   A man that all his time
Hath founded his good fortunes on your love,
Shared dangers with you—
Oth. The handkerchief!
Des. In sooth, you are to blame. 110
Oth. Away!   *Exit.*
Emil. Is not this man jealous?
Des. I ne'er saw this before.
Sure there's some wonder in this handkerchief.
I am most unhappy in the loss of it. 115
Emil. 'Tis not a year or two shows us a man.
They are all but stomachs, and we all but food;
They eat us hungerly, and when they are full,
They belch us.

136-37. **shut myself up in some other course,/ To fortune's alms:** be resigned to another way of life dependent on such slight means as Fortune may dole out

138. **thrice-gentle:** made gentle by the conditions of his nature, birth, and breeding; see **thrice-driven,** I. iii. 250.

139. **My advocation is not now in tune:** my pleading is not opportune at the moment.

141. **favor:** face; see II. i. 261.

144. **blank:** the white center of a target

Enter *Iago* and *Cassio*.

           Look you—Cassio and my husband!   120
  Iago. There is no other way; 'tis she must do't.
And lo the happiness! Go and importune her.
  Des. How now, good Cassio? What's the news with
    you?
  Cas. Madam, my former suit. I do beseech you   125
That by your virtuous means I may again
Exist, and be a member of his love
Whom I with all the office of my heart
Entirely honor. I would not be delayed.
If my offense be of such mortal kind   ·   130
That neither service past, nor present sorrows,
Nor purposed merit in futurity,
Can ransom me into his love again,
But to know so must be my benefit.
So shall I clothe me in a forced content,   135
And shut myself up in some other course,
To fortune's alms.
  Des.   '   Alas, thrice-gentle Cassio!
My advocation is not now in tune.
My lord is not my lord; nor should I know him,   140
Were he in favor as in humor altered.
So help me every spirit sanctified
As I have spoken for you all my best
And stood within the blank of his displeasure
For my free speech! You must awhile be patient.   145
What I can do I will; and more I will
Than for myself I dare. Let that suffice you.
  Iago. Is my lord angry?

158. **Something . . . of state:** business of state

159. **unhatched practice:** unexecuted plot

164. **endues:** endows

167. **of:** from; **observancy:** consideration

168. **Beshrew me:** literally, "curse me"; actually a mild expression.

169. **unhandsome:** unfair in the sense of being unsportsmanlike. Desdemona probably remembers Othello's salutation, "O, my fair warrior," II. i. 210.

170. **Arraigning his unkindness with my soul:** charging his unkindness for my soul's judgment

171. **I had suborned the witness:** literally, "caused the witness to commit perjury"; that is, deliberately misconstrued the meaning of the evidence

174. **toy:** whim

Emil.   He went hence but now,
And certainly in strange unquietness.   150
  Iago. Can he be angry? I have seen the cannon
When it hath blown his ranks into the air
And, like the devil, from his very arm
Puffed his own brother—and can he be angry?
Something of moment then. I will go meet him.   155
There's matter in't indeed if he be angry.
  Des. I prithee do so.

                                           Exit [Iago].
                    Something sure of state,
Either from Venice or some unhatched practice
Made demonstrable here in Cyprus to him,   160
Hath puddled his clear spirit; and in such cases
Men's natures wrangle with inferior things,
Though great ones are their object. 'Tis even so.
For let our finger ache, and it endues
Our other healthful members even to that sense   165
Of pain. Nay, we must think men are not gods,
Nor of them look for such observancy
As fits the bridal. Beshrew me much, Emilia,
I was (unhandsome warrior as I am!)
Arraigning his unkindness with my soul;   170
But now I find I had suborned the witness,
And he's indicted falsely.
  Emil. Pray heaven it be state matters, as you think,
And no conception nor no jealous toy
Concerning you.   175
  Des. Alas the day! I never gave him cause.
  Emil. But jealous souls will not be answered so.
They are not ever jealous for the cause,

188. **What make you**: what are you doing.

194. **dial**: a full circuit of the clock's hands

199. **Strike off this score of absence**: settle the debt you have been recording

200. **Take me this work out**: copy this embroidery for me; see III. iii. 334.

But jealous for they are jealous. 'Tis a monster
Begot upon itself, born on itself.   180
    Des. Heaven keep that monster from Othello's mind!
    Emil. Lady, amen.
    Des. I will go seek him. Cassio, walk here about.
If I do find him fit, I'll move your suit
And seek to effect it to my uttermost.   185
    Cas. I humbly thank your ladyship.
                    Exeunt Desdemona and Emilia.

              Enter *Bianca.*

    Bian. Save you, friend Cassio!
    Cas.   What make you from home?
How is it with you, my most fair Bianca?
I' faith, sweet love, I was coming to your house.   190
    Bian. And I was going to your lodging, Cassio.
What, keep a week away? seven days and nights?
Eightscore eight hours? and lovers' absent hours,
More tedious than the dial eightscore times?
O weary reck'ning!   195
    Cas.   Pardon me, Bianca.
I have this while with leaden thoughts been pressed;
But I shall in a more convenient time
Strike off this score of absence. Sweet Bianca,
            [Gives her Desdemona's handkerchief.]
Take me this work out.   200
    Bian.   O Cassio, whence came this?
This is some token from a newer friend.
To the felt absence now I feel a cause.
Is't come to this? Well, well.

217. **addition**: credit
222. **bring**: escort
223. **soon at night**: this very night
226. **I must be circumstanced**: I must accept circumstances.

Cas.   Go to, woman!   205
Throw your vile guesses in the devil's teeth,
From whence you have them. You are jealous now
That this is from some mistress, some remembrance.
No, by my faith, Bianca.
    Bian.   Why, whose is it?   210
    Cas. I know not, sweet. I found it in my chamber.
I like the work well. Ere it be demanded,
As like enough it will, I would have it copied.
Take it and do't, and leave me for this time.
    Bian. Leave you? Wherefore?   215
    Cas. I do attend here on the General
And think it no addition, nor my wish,
To have him see me womaned.
    Bian.   Why, I pray you?
    Cas. Not that I love you not.   220
    Bian.   But that you do not love me!
I pray you bring me on the way a little,
And say if I shall see you soon at night.
    Cas. 'Tis but a little way that I can bring you,
For I attend here; but I'll see you soon.   225
    Bian. 'Tis very good. I must be circumstanced.
                        Exeunt.

THE TRAGEDY OF

OTHELLO,

THE MOOR OF VENICE

ACT IV

IV. i. Iago continues to feed Othello's jealousy with pictures of Desdemona's infidelity. Othello, beside himself, falls in a faint. Iago then contrives to have Cassio talk of Bianca while Othello, hiding within earshot, believes that Cassio's words apply to Desdemona.

Desdemona enters with Lodovico, an emissary from the Duke of Venice, who brings a message recalling Othello to Venice and placing Cassio in command at Cyprus. Enraged by Desdemona's innocent reaction, which he misinterprets, Othello strikes Desdemona and sends her away. Alone with Lodovico, Iago insinuates that Othello is much changed for the worse, a suggestion that Lodovico finds easy to believe in the light of what he has just seen.

<hr>

9. **hypocrisy against the devil:** behaving with the appearance of wickedness but without wicked intent

ACT IV

Scene I. [Cyprus. Before the Castle.]

Enter *Othello* and *Iago*.

Iago. Will you think so?
Oth.   Think so, Iago?
Iago.   What,
To kiss in private?
Oth.   An unauthorized kiss.   5
Iago. Or to be naked with her friend in bed
An hour, or more, not meaning any harm?
Oth. Naked in bed, Iago, and not mean harm?
It is hypocrisy against the devil.
They that mean virtuously, and yet do so,   10
The devil their virtue tempts, and they tempt heaven.
Iago. So they do nothing, 'tis a venial slip.
But if I give my wife a handkerchief—
Oth. What then?
Iago. Why, then 'tis hers, my lord; and being hers,   15
She may, I think, bestow't on any man.
Oth. She is protectress of her honor too.
May she give that?

20. **They have it very oft that have it not:** Iago is saying that honor is merely a matter of reputation.

25. **Boding:** portentous

30. **as knaves be such abroad:** since there are such knaves

33. **Convinced or supplied:** seduced or satisfied

48-50. **Nature would not invest herself in such shadowing passion without some instruction:** my natural state of mind would not be so disrupted without some truthful premonition.

Iago. Her honor is an essence that's not seen;
They have it very oft that have it not.   20
But for the handkerchief—
   Oth. By heaven, I would most gladly have forgot it!
Thou said'st (O, it comes o'er my memory
As doth the raven o'er the infected house,
Boding to all!) he had my handkerchief.   25
   Iago. Ay, what of that?
   Oth.   That's not so good now.
   Iago.   What
If I had said I had seen him do you wrong?
Or heard him say—as knaves be such abroad   30
Who having, by their own importunate suit,
Or voluntary dotage of some mistress,
Convinced or supplied them, cannot choose
But they must blab—
   Oth.   Hath he said anything?   35
   Iago. He hath, my lord; but be you well assured,
No more than he'll unswear.
   Oth.   What hath he said?
   Iago. Faith, that he did—I know not what he did.
   Oth. What? what?   40
   Iago. Lie—
   Oth.   With her?
   Iago.   With her, on her; what you will.
   Oth. Lie with her? lie on her?—We say lie on her when
they belie her.—Lie with her! Zounds, that's fulsome.   45
—Handkerchief—confessions—handkerchief!—To confess,
and be hanged for his labor—first to be hanged, and
then to confess! I tremble at it. Nature would not invest
herself in such shadowing passion without some instruc-

69. **on great occasion:** about something important

71. **Dost thou mock me:** the thought of Desdemona's infidelity is so prevalent in Othello's mind that the reference to his head makes him think of a cuckold's horns.

76. **civil:** civilized

tion. It is not words that shakes me thus.—Pish! Noses,   50
ears, and lips? Is't possible?—Confess?—handkerchief?—
O devil!   *Falls in a trance.*
  Iago. Work on,
My medicine, work! Thus credulous fools are caught,
And many worthy and chaste dames even thus,   55
All guiltless, meet reproach.—What, ho! my lord!
My lord, I say! Othello!

                    Enter *Cassio.*

                    How now, Cassio?
  Cas. What's the matter?
  Iago. My lord is fall'n into an epilepsy.   60
This is his second fit; he had one yesterday.
  Cas. Rub him about the temples.
  Iago.   No, forbear.
The lethargy must have his quiet course.
If not, he foams at mouth, and by-and-by   65
Breaks out to savage madness. Look, he stirs.
Do you withdraw yourself a little while.
He will recover straight. When he is gone,
I would on great occasion speak with you.
                                    [*Exit Cassio.*]
How is it, General? Have you not hurt your head?   70
  Oth. Dost thou mock me?
  Iago.   I mock you? No, by heaven.
Would you would bear your fortune like a man!
  Oth. A horned man's a monster and a beast.
  Iago. There's many a beast then in a populous city, 75
And many a civil monster.
  Oth. Did he confess it?

79-80. **every bearded fellow that's but yoked/ May draw with you:** every mature man needs only to be yoked (like a draft animal) to pull the same burden; that is, all mature men are in the same boat with you.

81-2. **those unproper beds/ Which they dare swear peculiar:** beds which are not exclusively reserved for them, though they would swear otherwise. Peculiar means "exclusive."

84. **secure:** carefree

89. **in a patient list:** within the limits of patience

91. **passion:** fit

92. **shifted him away:** got him away on a pretext

93. **ecstasy:** trance

95. **encave:** hide

96. **fleers:** contemptuous looks, synonymous with gibes and scorns

100. **cope:** meet in amorous contest

101. **gesture:** behavior; **Marry:** an interjection

102. **all in all in spleen:** all spleen; completely controlled by rage

108. **keep time:** measure your actions and behave reasonably.

Iago.   Good sir, be a man.
Think every bearded fellow that's but yoked
May draw with you. There's millions now alive   80
That nightly lie in those unproper beds
Which they dare swear peculiar. Your case is better.
O, 'tis the spite of hell, the fiend's arch-mock,
To lip a wanton in a secure couch,
And to suppose her chaste! No, let me know;   85
And knowing what I am, I know what she shall be.
    Oth. O, thou art wise! 'Tis certain.
    Iago.   Stand you awhile apart;
Confine yourself but in a patient list.
Whilst you were here, o'erwhelmed with your grief   90
(A passion most unfitting such a man),
Cassio came hither. I shifted him away
And laid good 'scuse upon your ecstasy;
Bade him anon return, and here speak with me;
The which he promised. Do but encave yourself   95
And mark the fleers, the gibes, and notable scorns
That dwell in every region of his face;
For I will make him tell the tale anew—
Where, how, how oft, how long ago, and when
He hath, and is again to cope your wife.   100
I say, but mark his gesture. Marry, patience!
Or I shall say you are all in all in spleen,
And nothing of a man.
    Oth.   Dost thou hear, Iago?
I will be found most cunning in my patience;   105
But (dost thou hear?) most bloody.
    Iago.   That's not amiss;
But yet keep time in all. Will you withdraw?
                          [*Othello retires.*]

110. **huswife:** hussy

117. **unbookish:** unlearned, ignorant of the truth; **conster:** construe, interpret

120. **addition:** title

125. **caitiff:** "wretch," used in pity rather than contempt

136. **Roman:** "proud conqueror," probably used because of the familiarity of the conception of a Roman triumph

137-38. **customer:** prostitute; **bear some charity to my wit:** allow me some credit for wisdom.

Now will I question Cassio of Bianca,
A huswife that by selling her desires   110
Buys herself bread and clothes. It is a creature
That dotes on Cassio, as 'tis the strumpet's plague
To beguile many and be beguiled by one.
He, when he hears of her, cannot refrain
From the excess of laughter. Here he comes.   115

Enter *Cassio*.

As he shall smile, Othello shall go mad;
And his unbookish jealousy must conster
Poor Cassio's smiles, gestures, and light behavior
Quite in the wrong. How do you now, Lieutenant?
  Cas. The worser that you give me the addition   120
Whose want even kills me.
  Iago. Ply Desdemona well, and you are sure on't.
Now, if this suit lay in Bianca's power,
How quickly should you speed!
  Cas.   Alas, poor caitiff!   125
  Oth. Look how he laughs already!
  Iago. I never knew woman love man so.
  Cas. Alas, poor rogue! I think, i' faith, she loves me.
  Oth. Now he denies it faintly, and laughs it out.
  Iago. Do you hear, Cassio?   130
  Oth.   Now he importunes him
To tell it o'er. Go to! Well said, well said!
  Iago. She gives it out that you shall marry her.
Do you intend it?
  Cas. Ha, ha, ha!   135
  Oth. Do you triumph, Roman? Do you triumph?
  Cas. I marry her? What, a customer? Prithee bear some

140. **Laugh that wins**: "let the winner laugh," proverbial.

141. **the cry goes**: rumor has it

144. **Have you scored me**: almost equivalent to modern slang: "Have you scored on me?"

151. **bauble**: toy, plaything

162. **such another**: such a (emphatic); **fitchew**: polecat; also slang for whore; **marry**: an interjection; see IV. i. 101; **a perfumed one**: that is, one who attempts to conceal by artifice her real nature

charity to my wit; do not think it so unwholesome. Ha,
ha, ha!

Oth. So, so, so, so! Laugh that wins! 140

Iago. Faith, the cry goes that you shall marry her.

Cas. Prithee say true.

Iago. I am a very villain else.

Oth. Have you scored me? Well.

Cas. This is the monkey's own giving out. She is per- 145
suaded I will marry her out of her own love and flattery,
not out of my promise.

Oth. Iago beckons me. Now he begins the story.

Cas. She was here even now; she haunts me in every
place. I was t'other day talking on the sea bank with cer- 150
tain Venetians, and thither comes the bauble, and, by this
hand, she falls me thus about my neck—

Oth. Crying "O dear Cassio!" as it were. His gesture
imports it.

Cas. So hangs, and lolls, and weeps upon me; so hales 155
and pulls me! Ha, ha, ha!

Oth. Now he tells how she plucked him to my chamber.
O, I see that nose of yours, but not that dog I shall throw't
to.

Cas. Well, I must leave her company. 160

Enter *Bianca*.

Iago. Before me! Look where she comes.

Cas. 'Tis such another fitchew! marry, a perfumed one.
What do you mean by this haunting of me?

Bian. Let the devil and his dam haunt you! What did
you mean by that same handkerchief you gave me even 165
now? I was a fine fool to take it. I must take out the

170. **hobbyhorse:** originally the wooden horse ridden by a performer in the May Day morris dance; hence, a plaything. Bianca here means the new mistress she suspects Cassio of keeping.

174. **should:** must

176. **when you are next prepared for:** never

181-82. **would very fain:** am very eager to

work? A likely piece of work that you should find it in
your chamber and know not who left it there! This is
some minx's token, and I must take out the work? There!
give it your hobbyhorse. Wheresoever you had it, I'll take 170
out no work on't.

Cas. How now, my sweet Bianca? How now? how
now?

Oth. By heaven, that should be my handkerchief!

Bian. An you'll come to supper tonight, you may; an 175
you will not, come when you are next prepared for. *Exit.*

Iago. After her, after her!

Cas. Faith, I must; she'll rail i' the street else.

Iago. Will you sup there?

Cas. Yes, I intend so.   180

Iago. Well, I may chance to see you; for I would very
fain speak with you.

Cas. Prithee come. Will you?

Iago. Go to! say no more.

                                        Exit Cassio.

Oth. [*Comes forward*] How shall I murder him, Iago? 185

Iago. Did you perceive how he laughed at his vice?

Oth. O Iago!

Iago. And did you see the handkerchief?

Oth. Was that mine?

Iago. Yours, by this hand! And to see how he prizes 190
the foolish woman your wife! She gave it him, and he
hath giv'n it his whore.

Oth. I would have him nine years a-killing!—A fine
woman! a fair woman! a sweet woman!

Iago. Nay, you must forget that.   195

Oth. Ay, let her rot, and perish, and be damned tonight, for she shall not live. No, my heart is turned to

201. **not your way**: not the way you must behave
208. **condition**: temperament
212. **fond**: foolish; see II. i. 157.
213. **patent**: license
225. **let me be his undertaker**: **undertaker** did not mean funeral director in Elizabethan times. Iago merely means that he will "settle his hash."

stone: I strike it, and it hurts my hand. O, the world hath
not a sweeter creature! She might lie by an emperor's side
and command him tasks.   200

Iago. Nay, that's not your way.

Oth. Hang her! I do but say what she is. So delicate
with her needle! an admirable musician! O, she will sing
the savageness out of a bear! Of so high and plenteous wit
and invention!   205

Iago. She's the worse for all this.

Oth. O, a thousand thousand times! And then, of so
gentle a condition!

Iago. Ay, too gentle.

Oth. Nay, that's certain. But yet the pity of it, Iago! O 210
Iago, the pity of it, Iago!

Iago. If you are so fond over her iniquity, give her
patent to offend; for if it touch not you, it comes near
nobody.

Oth. I will chop her into messes! Cuckold me!   215

Iago. O, 'tis foul in her.

Oth. With mine officer!

Iago. That's fouler.

Oth. Get me some poison, Iago, this night. I'll not ex-
postulate with her, lest her body and beauty unprovide   220
my mind again. This night, Iago!

Iago. Do it not with poison. Strangle her in her bed,
even the bed she hath contaminated.

Oth. Good, good! The justice of it pleases. Very good!

Iago. And for Cassio, let me be his undertaker. You   225
shall hear more by midnight.

Oth. Excellent good!   *A trumpet.*
                 What trumpet is that same?

Iago. Something from Venice, sure.

233. **With all my heart:** amen.

235. **the instrument:** the letter. This is formal courtesy; not meant literally.

249. **atone:** reconcile

Enter *Lodovico, Desdemona,* and *Attendants.*

                                  'Tis Lodovico,   230
Come from the Duke; and see, your wife is with him.
  Lod. God save you, worthy General!
  Oth.   With all my heart, sir.
  Lod. The Duke and Senators of Venice greet you.
                        [*Gives him a letter.*]
  Oth. I kiss the instrument of their pleasures.   235
                   [*Opens the letter and reads.*]
  Des. And what's the news, good cousin Lodovico?
  Iago. I am very glad to see you, signior.
Welcome to Cyprus.
  Lod. I thank you. How does Lieutenant Cassio?
  Iago.   Lives, sir.   240
  Des. Cousin, there's fall'n between him and my lord
An unkind breach; but you shall make all well.
  Oth. Are you sure of that?
  Des. My lord?
  Oth. [*Reads*] "This fail you not to do, as you will—" 245
  Lod. He did not call; he's busy in the paper.
Is there division 'twixt thy lord and Cassio?
  Des. A most unhappy one. I would do much
T' atone them, for the love I bear to Cassio.
  Oth. Fire and brimstone!   250
  Des.   My lord?
  Oth.   Are you wise?
  Des. What, is he angry?
  Lod.   May be the letter moved him;
For, as I think, they do command him home,   255
Deputing Cassio in his government.

268. **teem:** conceive

279. **she can turn, and turn, and yet go on:** she twists and turns to conceal the real direction of her movement, but so skillfully that she nevertheless always moves toward her secret goals; in other words, she is adept at deception.

Des. By my troth, I am glad on't.

Oth.   Indeed?

Des.   My lord?

Oth. I am glad to see you mad.   260

Des.   Why, sweet Othello!

Oth. Devil!   [*Strikes her.*]

Des. I have not deserved this.

Lod. My lord, this would not be believed in Venice,
Though I should swear I saw't. 'Tis very much.   265
Make her amends; she weeps.

Oth.   O devil, devil!
If that the earth could teem with woman's tears,
Each drop she falls would prove a crocodile.
Out of my sight!   270

Des.   I will not stay to offend you.   [*Going.*]

Lod. Truly, an obedient lady.
I do beseech your lordship call her back.

Oth. Mistress!

Des.   My lord?   275

Oth.   What would you with her, sir?

Lod. Who? I, my lord?

Oth. Ay! You did wish that I would make her turn.
Sir, she can turn, and turn, and yet go on,
And turn again; and she can weep, sir, weep;   280
And she's obedient; as you say, obedient,
Very obedient.—Proceed you in your tears.—
Concerning this, sir (O well-painted passion!),
I am commanded home.—Get you away;
I'll send for you anon.—Sir, I obey the mandate   285
And will return to Venice.—Hence, avaunt!

                    [*Exit Desdemona.*]

297. **that**: what; **censure**: judgment; see II. [iii.] 195.

307. **honesty**: honorable action

Cassio shall have my place. And, sir, tonight
I do entreat that we may sup together.
You are welcome, sir, to Cyprus.—Goats and monkeys!

Exit.

   Lod. Is this the noble Moor whom our full senate   290
Call all in all sufficient? Is this the nature
Whom passion could not shake? whose solid virtue
The shot of accident nor dart of chance
Could neither graze nor pierce?

   Iago.   He is much changed.   295
   Lod. Are his wits safe? Is he not light of brain?
   Iago. He's that he is. I may not breathe my censure.
What he might be—if what he might he is not—
I would to heaven he were!

   Lod.   What, strike his wife?   300
   Iago. Faith, that was not so well; yet would I knew
That stroke would prove the worst!

   Lod.   Is it his use?
Or did the letters work upon his blood
And new-create this fault?   305

   Iago.   Alas, alas!
It is not honesty in me to speak
What I have seen and known. You shall observe him,
And his own courses will denote him so
That I may save my speech. Do but go after   310
And mark how he continues.

   Lod. I am sorry that I am deceived in him.

Exeunt.

IV. ii. Othello questions Emilia, who stoutly affirms Desdemona's innocence, but Othello refuses to believe her and reviles Desdemona to her face as a common whore. Desdemona, bewildered and crushed, appeals to Iago for an explanation and Emilia suggests that some "busy and insinuating rogue" has devised the slander.

Roderigo comes to complain to Iago that he has had no notice from Desdemona, despite his many gifts supposedly delivered by Iago. Iago soothes him and tells him that the only way to prevent Othello's departure with Desdemona is to kill Cassio that night.

⁣⁣⁣⁣⁣⁣⁣⁣⁣⁣⁣⁣⁣⁣⁣⁣⁣⁣⁣⁣⁣⁣⁣⁣⁣⁣⁣⁣⁣

10. **mask**: when they went out in public, fashionable Elizabethan ladies sometimes wore masks covering the eyes.

18. **the serpent's curse**: the curse laid on the snake who beguiled Eve

20. **happy**: fortunate

23-4. **she's a simple bawd/ That cannot say as much**: any bawd would have as much skill in dissimulation. Othello considers that Emilia must have been a go-between to assist Desdemona in her infidelity.

25. **closet**: private chamber

Scene II. [Cyprus. Within the Castle.]

Enter *Othello* and *Emilia.*

Oth. You have seen nothing then?
Emil. Nor ever heard, nor ever did suspect.
Oth. Yes, you have seen Cassio and she together.
Emil. But then I saw no harm, and then I heard
Each syllable that breath made up between them.   5
Oth. What, did they never whisper?
Emil.   Never, my lord.
Oth. Nor send you out o' the way?
Emil. Never.
Oth. To fetch her fan, her gloves, her mask, nor noth-   10
    ing?
Emil. Never, my lord.
Oth. That's strange.
Emil. I durst, my lord, to wager she is honest,
Lay down my soul at stake. If you think other,   15
Remove your thought; it doth abuse your bosom.
If any wretch have put this in your head,
Let heaven requite it with the serpent's cursel
For if she be not honest, chaste, and true,
There's no man happy; the purest of their wives   20
Is foul as slander.
Oth.   Bid her come hither. Go.
                                    Exit Emilia.
She says enough; yet she's a simple bawd
That cannot say as much. This is a subtle whore,
A closet lock and key of villainous secrets;   25
And yet she'll kneel and pray; I have seen her do't.

33-6. Some . . . mystery: Othello is pretending that Desdemona is a prostitute and Emilia her bawd. **Your mystery, your mystery:** that is, perform your office (as a bawd).

52. **motive:** mover, the one who sets them in motion

Enter *Desdemona* and *Emilia*.

Des. My lord, what is your will?
Oth.   Pray, chuck, come hither.
Des. What is your pleasure?
Oth.   Let me see your eyes.   30
Look in my face.
   Des.   What horrible fancy's this?
   Oth. [*To Emilia*] Some of your function, mistress.
Leave procreants alone and shut the door;
Cough or cry hem if anybody come.   35
Your mystery, your mystery! Nay, dispatch!
                        Exit Emilia.
   Des. Upon my knees, what doth your speech import?
I understand a fury in your words,
But not the words.
   Oth. Why, what art thou?   40
   Des.   Your wife, my lord; your true
And loyal wife.
   Oth.   Come, swear it, damn thyself;
Lest, being like one of heaven, the devils themselves
Should fear to seize thee. Therefore be double-damned—   45
Swear thou art honest.
   Des.   Heaven doth truly know it.
   Oth. Heaven truly knows that thou art false as hell.
   Des. To whom, my lord? With whom? How am I false?
   Oth. Ah, Desdemon! away! away! away!   50
   Des. Alas the heavy day! Why do you weep?
Am I the motive of these tears, my lord?
If haply you my father do suspect
An instrument of this your calling back,

64. **time of scorn:** scornful time

67. **there:** that is, his love for Desdemona

72-3. **turn thy complexion there,/ Patience:** let that be the limit of composure.

76. **shambles:** slaughterhouse

77. **quicken:** are conceived; see III. iii. 312.

84. **commoner:** prostitute

Lay not your blame on me. If you have lost him,   55
Why, I have lost him too.
    Oth.   Had it pleased heaven
To try me with affliction, had they rained
All kinds of sores and shames on my bare head,
Steeped me in poverty to the very lips,   60
Given to captivity me and my utmost hopes,
I should have found in some place of my soul
A drop of patience. But, alas, to make me
A fixed figure for the time of scorn
To point his slow and moving finger at!   65
Yet could I bear that too; well, very well.
But there where I have garnered up my heart,
Where either I must live or bear no life,
The fountain from the which my current runs
Or else dries up—to be discarded thence,   70
Or keep it as a cistern for foul toads
To knot and gender in—turn thy complexion there,
Patience, thou young and rose-lipped cherubin!
I here look grim as hell!
    Des. I hope my noble lord esteems me honest.   75
    Oth. O, ay! as summer flies are in the shambles,
That quicken even with blowing. O thou weed,
Who art so lovely fair, and smell'st so sweet,
That the sense aches at thee, would thou hadst ne'er been
    born!   80
    Des. Alas, what ignorant sin have I committed?
    Oth. Was this fair paper, this most goodly book,
Made to write "whore" upon? What committed?
Committed? O thou public commoner!
I should make very forges of my cheeks   85
That would to cinders burn up modesty,

90. **hollow mine of earth**: the interior of the earth was believed to be hollow and the home of the winds.

103. **cry you mercy**: beg your pardon

Did I but speak thy deeds. What committed?
Heaven stops the nose at it, and the moon winks;
The bawdy wind, that kisses all it meets,
Is hushed within the hollow mine of earth   90
And will not hear it. What committed?
Impudent strumpet!
   Des.   By heaven, you do me wrong!
   Oth. Are not you a strumpet?
   Des.   No, as I am a Christian!   95
If to preserve this vessel for my lord
From any other foul unlawful touch
Be not to be a strumpet, I am none.
   Oth. What, not a whore?
   Des.   No, as I shall be saved!   100
   Oth. Is't possible?
   Des. O, heaven forgive us!
   Oth.   I cry you mercy then.
I took you for that cunning whore of Venice
That married with Othello.—You, mistress,   105
That have the office opposite to Saint Peter
And keep the gate of hell!

Enter *Emilia.*

               You, you, ay, you!
We have done our course. There's money for your pains.
I pray you turn the key, and keep our counsel.   *Exit.* 110
   Emil. Alas, what does this gentleman conceive?
How do you, madam? How do you, my good lady?
   Des. Faith, half asleep.
   Emil. Good madam, what's the matter with my lord?
   Des. With who?   115

121. **water:** tears

125. **meet:** fitting

126-27. **How have I been behaved, that he might stick/ The small'st opinion on my least misuse:** what have I done that he should find even the slightest cause to suspect me of any misconduct.

142. **callet:** female vagabond

Emil. Why, with my lord, madam.

Des. Who is thy lord?

Emil.   He that is yours, sweet lady.

Des. I have none. Do not talk to me, Emilia.
I cannot weep; nor answer have I none   120
But what should go by water. Prithee tonight
Lay on my bed my wedding sheets, remember;
And call thy husband hither.

Emil.   Here's a change indeed! *Exit.*

Des. 'Tis meet I should be used so, very meet.   125
How have I been behaved, that he might stick
The small'st opinion on my least misuse?

Enter *Iago* and *Emilia.*

Iago. What is your pleasure, madam? How is't with
    you?

Des. I cannot tell. Those that do teach young babes   130
Do it with gentle means and easy tasks.
He might have chid me so; for, in good faith,
I am a child to chiding.

Iago.   What is the matter, lady?

Emil. Alas, Iago, my lord hath so bewhored her,   135
Thrown such despite and heavy terms upon her
As true hearts cannot bear.

Des. Am I that name, Iago?

Iago.   What name, fair lady?

Des. Such as she says my lord did say I was.   140

Emil. He called her whore. A beggar in his drink
Could not have laid such terms upon his callet.

Iago. Why did he so?

Des. I do not know. I am sure I am none such.

151. **trick:** caprice
155. **cogging:** cheating, synonymous with **cozening**
168. **Speak within door:** watch your tongue; don't speak so wildly.

Iago. Do not weep, do not weep. Alas the day!   145
   Emil. Hath she forsook so many noble matches,
Her father and her country, all her friends,
To be called whore? Would it not make one weep?
   Des. It is my wretched fortune.
   Iago.   Beshrew him for't!   150
How comes this trick upon him?
   Des.   Nay, heaven doth know.
   Emil. I will be hanged if some eternal villain,
Some busy and insinuating rogue,
Some cogging, cozening slave, to get some office,   155
Have not devised this slander. I'll be hanged else.
   Iago. Fie, there is no such man! It is impossible.
   Des. If any such there be, heaven pardon him!
   Emil. A halter pardon him! and hell gnaw his bones!
Why should he call her whore? Who keeps her company?   160
What place? what time? what form? what likelihood?
The Moor's abused by some most villainous knave,
Some base notorious knave, some scurvy fellow.
O heaven, that such companions thou'dst unfold,
And put in every honest hand a whip   165
To lash the rascals naked through the world
Even from the East to the West!
   Iago.   Speak within door.
   Emil. O, fie upon them! Some such squire he was
That turned your wit the seamy side without   170
And made you to suspect me with the Moor.
   Iago. You are a fool. Go to.
   Des.   O good Iago,
What shall I do to win my lord again?
Good friend, go to him; for, by this light of heaven,   175
I know not how I lost him. Here I kneel.

179, 181. **that:** if .
188. **addition:** title; see IV. i. 120.
190. **be content:** don't be upset.
196. **stay the meat:** stay to dine
201. **daff'st me:** doff me; put me off
203. **conveniency:** opportunity

If e'er my will did trespass 'gainst his love
Either in discourse of thought or actual deed,
Or that mine eyes, mine ears, or any sense
Delighted them in any other form,   180
Or that I do not yet, and ever did,
And ever will (though he do shake me off
To beggarly divorcement) love him dearly,
Comfort forswear me! Unkindness may do much;
And his unkindness may defeat my life,   185
But never taint my love. I cannot say "whore."
It doth abhor me now I speak the word;
To do the act that might th' addition earn
Not the world's mass of vanity could make me.

 Iago. I pray you be content. 'Tis but his humor.   190
The business of the state does him offense,
And he does chide with you.

 Des. If 'twere no other—

 Iago.   'Tis but so, I warrant.

         [*Trumpets within.*]

Hark how these instruments summon you to supper.   195
The messengers of Venice stay the meat.
Go in, and weep not. All things shall be well.

      Exeunt Desdemona and Emilia.

    Enter *Roderigo.*

How now, Roderigo?

 Rod. I do not find that thou deal'st justly with me.

 Iago. What in the contrary?   200

 Rod. Every day thou daff'st me with some device,
Iago, and rather, as it seems to me now, keep'st from me
all conveniency than suppliest me with the least ad-

205. **put up in peace:** overlook; put away and forget

213. **votarist:** nun

220. **fopped:** made a fool of

226. **You have said now:** you've said all that needs to be said.

vantage of hope. I will indeed no longer endure it; nor
am I yet persuaded to put up in peace what already I 205
have foolishly suffered.

Iago. Will you hear me, Roderigo?

Rod. Faith, I have heard too much; for your words and
performances are no kin together.

Iago. You charge me most unjustly. 210

Rod. With naught but truth. I have wasted myself out
of means. The jewels you have had from me to deliver to
Desdemona would half have corrupted a votarist. You
have told me she hath received them, and returned me
expectations and comforts of sudden respect and ac- 215
quaintance; but I find none.

Iago. Well, go to; very well.

Rod. Very well! go to! I cannot go to, man; nor 'tis not
very well. Nay, I think it is scurvy, and begin to find myself fopped in it. 220

Iago. Very well.

Rod. I tell you 'tis not very well. I will make myself
known to Desdemona. If she will return me my jewels,
I will give over my suit and repent my unlawful solicita-
tion. If not, assure yourself I will seek satisfaction of you. 225

Iago. You have said now.

Rod. Ay, and said nothing but what I protest intend-
ment of doing.

Iago. Why, now I see there's mettle in thee; and even
from this instant do build on thee a better opinion than 230
ever before. Give me thy hand, Roderigo. Thou hast taken
against me a most just exception; but yet I protest I have
dealt most directly in thy affair.

Rod. It hath not appeared.

Iago. I grant indeed it hath not appeared; and your 235

241. **engines for**: ingenious contrivances against
249-50. **none can be so determinate**: no consideration can have as much effect
256. **harlotry**: harlot
261. **amazed**: dumfounded
264-65. **grows to waste**: is wasting, passing

suspicion is not without wit and judgment. But, Roderigo,
if thou hast that in thee indeed which I have greater reason to believe now than ever (I mean purpose, courage,
and valor), this night show it. If thou the next night following enjoy not Desdemona, take me from this world 240
with treachery and devise engines for my life.

Rod. Well, what is it? Is it within reason and compass?

Iago. Sir, there is especial commission come from
Venice to depute Cassio in Othello's place.

Rod. Is that true? Why, then Othello and Desdemona 245
return again to Venice.

Iago. O, no. He goes into Mauritania and takes away
with him the fair Desdemona, unless his abode be lin-
gered here by some accident; wherein none can be so determinate as the removing of Cassio. 250

Rod. How do you mean removing of him?

Iago. Why, by making him uncapable of Othello's
place—knocking out his brains.

Rod. And that you would have me to do?

Iago. Ay, if you dare do yourself a profit and a right. 255
He sups tonight with a harlotry, and thither will I go to
him. He knows not yet of his honorable fortune. If you
will watch his going thence, which I will fashion to fall out
between twelve and one, you may take him at your pleasure. I will be near to second your attempt, and he shall 260
fall between us. Come, stand not amazed at it, but go
along with me. I will show you such a necessity in his
death that you shall think yourself bound to put it on
him. It is now high supper time, and the night grows to
waste. About it! 265

Rod. I will hear further reason for this.

Iago. And you shall be satisfied.　　　　　　*Exeunt.*

IV. iii. As Othello leaves to escort Lodovico from the Castle, he orders Desdemona to prepare at once for bed and to dismiss Emilia, for he will return in a short time. Desdemona, full of foreboding, expresses her bewildered misery and sings the melancholy "Willow" song, which increases the atmosphere of impending catastrophe.

||||||||||||||||||||||||||||||||||||||

13. **incontinent:** immediately; see I. iii. 330.
22. **stubbornness:** harshness
25. **All's one:** it doesn't matter.

Scene III. [Cyprus. Another room in the Castle.]

Enter *Othello, Lodovico, Desdemona, Emilia,*
and *Attendants.*

Lod. I do beseech you, sir, trouble yourself no further.
Oth. O, pardon me; 'twill do me good to walk.
Lod. Madam, good night. I humbly thank your lady-
ship.
Des. Your Honor is most welcome.   5
Oth.   Will you walk, sir?
O, Desdemona—
Des. My lord?
Oth. Get you to bed on th' instant. I will be returned
forthwith. Dismiss your attendant there. Look't be done. 10
Des. I will, my lord.
              Exeunt [*Othello, Lodovico, and Attendants*].
Emil. How goes it now? He looks gentler than he did.
Des. He says he will return incontinent.
He hath commanded me to go to bed,
And bid me to dismiss you.   15
Emil.   Dismiss me?
Des. It was his bidding. Therefore, good Emilia,
Give me my nightly wearing, and adieu.
We must not now displease him.
Emil. I would you had never seen him!   20
Des. So would not I. My love doth so approve him
That even his stubbornness, his checks, his frowns
(Prithee unpin me) have grace and favor in them.
Emil. I have laid those sheets you bade me on the bed.
Des. All's one. Good faith, how foolish are our minds!   25

34-5. **I have much to do/ But to go hang my head:**
I can hardly keep from hanging my head.

If I do die before thee, prithee shroud me
In one of those same sheets.
    Emil.   Come, come! You talk.
    Des. My mother had a maid called Barbary.
She was in love; and he she loved proved mad   30
And did forsake her. She had a song of "Willow."
An old thing 'twas; but it expressed her fortune,
And she died singing it. That song tonight
Will not go from my mind. I have much to do
But to go hang my head all at one side   35
And sing it like poor Barbary. Prithee dispatch.
    Emil. Shall I go fetch your nightgown?
    Des.   No, unpin me here.
This Lodovico is a proper man.
    Emil. A very handsome man.   40
    Des. He speaks well.
    Emil. I know a lady in Venice would have walked
barefoot to Palestine for a touch of his nether lip.
    Des. (Sings)

> The poor soul sat sighing by a sycamore
>   tree,   45
>   Sing all a green willow:
> Her hand on her bosom, her head on her
>   knee,
>   Sing willow, willow, willow.
> The fresh streams ran by her and mur-   50
>   mured her moans;
>   Sing willow, willow, willow;
> Her salt tears fell from her, and soft'ned
>   the stones.
>   Sing willow—   55

58. **hie thee:** hurry

66. **mo:** more; see I. i. 182.

70. **'Tis neither here nor there:** it has no significance at all.

78. **by this heavenly light:** an oath, though Emilia replies facetiously

Lay by these.

> willow, willow;

Prithee hie thee; he'll come anon.

> Sing all a green willow must be my garland.
> Let nobody blame him; his scorn I approve— 60

Nay, that's not next. Hark! who is't that knocks?
  Emil. It is the wind.
  Des.

> I called my love false love; but what said
>   he then?
>   Sing willow, willow, willow: 65
> If I court mo women, you'll couch with
>   mo men.

So, get thee gone; good night. Mine eyes do itch.
Doth that bode weeping?
  Emil.   'Tis neither here nor there. 70
  Des. I have heard it said so. O, these men, these men!
Dost thou in conscience think—tell me, Emilia—
That there be women do abuse their husbands
In such gross kind?
  Emil.   There be some such, no question. 75
  Des. Wouldst thou do such a deed for all the world?
  Emil. Why, would not you?
  Des.   No, by this heavenly light!
  Emil. Nor I neither by this heavenly light.
I might do't as well i' the dark. 80
  Des. Wouldst thou do such a deed for all the world?

87. **joint-ring**: a traditional love token
88. **exhibition**: gift
89. **'Ud's pity**: by God's pity
98. **to the vantage**: in addition
103. **peevish**: foolish
105. **scant our former having**: decrease what we formerly had
106. **have galls**: are capable of resentment; **grace**: virtue
107. **revenge**: vengefulness

Emil. The world's a huge thing. It is a great price for
a small vice.

Des. In troth, I think thou wouldst not.

Emil. In troth, I think I should; and undo't when I   85
had done it. Marry, I would not do such a thing for a
joint-ring, nor for measures of lawn, nor for gowns, petti-
coats, nor caps, nor any petty exhibition; but, for all the
whole world—'Ud's pity! who would not make her husband a cuckold to make him a monarch? I should venture   90
purgatory for't.

Des. Beshrew me if I would do such a wrong
For the whole world.

Emil. Why, the wrong is but a wrong i' the world;
and having the world for your labor, 'tis a wrong in your   95
own world, and you might quickly make it right.

Des. I do not think there is any such woman.

Emil. Yes, a dozen; and as many to the vantage as
would store the world they played for.
But I do think it is their husbands' faults   100
If wives do fall. Say that they slack their duties
And pour our treasures into foreign laps;
Or else break out in peevish jealousies,
Throwing restraint upon us; or say they strike us,
Or scant our former having in despite—   105
Why, we have galls; and though we have some grace,
Yet have we some revenge. Let husbands know
Their wives have sense like them. They see, and smell,
And have their palates both for sweet and sour,
As husbands have. What is it that they do   110
When they change us for others? Is it sport?
I think it is. And doth affection breed it?
I think it doth. Is't frailty that thus errs?

118-20. **Heaven me such uses send,/ Not to pick bad from bad, but by bad mend**: heaven help me to avoid returning evil in kind but instead to, find self-improvement from it.

It is so too. And have not we affections,
Desires for sport, and frailty, as men have?   115
Then let them use us well; else let them know,
The ills we do, their ills instruct us so.
   Des. Good night, good night. Heaven me such uses
     send,
Not to pick bad from bad, but by bad mend!   120
                              Exeunt.

THE TRAGEDY OF

OTHELLO,

THE MOOR OF VENICE

ACT V

V. i. Iago, hoping to get rid of both Roderigo and Cassio, has induced Roderigo to attack Cassio from ambush. Cassio, however, wounds Roderigo and is himself unhurt until Iago slips up behind him and stabs him in the leg, fatally, he hopes. Othello enters briefly, observes Cassio wounded, and concludes that Iago has killed him as promised. In the darkened street, Iago manages to stab Roderigo to death. A crowd soon gathers, including Bianca, and Iago hints that she is involved in the plot on Cassio's life. The wounded Cassio is borne off. Realizing that all his plotting is nearing a climax, Iago remarks as the scene ends that "This is the night/ That either makes me or fordoes me quite."

▬▬▬▬▬▬▬▬▬▬

1. **bulk:** a projection from a building; e.g., the buttresses of a church; **straight:** immediately; see I. i. 151.
   12. **quat:** literally, "pimple," a term of contempt
   13. **sense:** quick
   18. **bobbed:** tricked

ACT V

Scene I. [Cyprus. A street.]

Enter Iago and Roderigo.

Iago. Here, stand behind this bulk; straight will he
  come.
Wear thy good rapier bare, and put it home.
Quick, quick! Fear nothing; I'll be at thy elbow.
It makes us, or it mars us—think on that,   5
And fix most firm thy resolution.
  Rod. Be near at hand. I may miscarry in't.
  Iago. Here, at thy hand. Be bold, and take thy stand.
                          [Stands aside.]
  Rod. I have no great devotion to the deed,
And yet he hath given me satisfying reasons.   10
'Tis but a man gone. Forth my sword! He dies!
  Iago. I have rubbed this young quat almost to the
  sense,
And he grows angry. Now whether he kill Cassio,
Or Cassio him, or each do kill the other,   15
Every way makes my gain. Live Roderigo,
He calls me to a restitution large
Of gold and jewels that I bobbed from him
As gifts to Desdemona.

23. **unfold me to him:** reveal my deceit to him
28. **make proof of:** try the virtue of
35. **brave:** noble, rather than courageous
37. **Minion:** darling (addressed to Desdemona)
39. **Forth of:** out of

It must not be. If Cassio do remain,   20
He hath a daily beauty in his life
That makes me ugly; and besides, the Moor
May unfold me to him; there stand I in much peril.
No, he must die. But so! I hear him coming.

Enter *Cassio*.

  Rod. I know his gait. 'Tis he. Villain, thou diest!   25
                              [*Makes a pass at Cassio.*]
  Cas. That thrust had been mine enemy indeed
But that my coat is better than thou know'st.
I will make proof of thine.
                              [*Draws, and wounds Roderigo.*]
  Rod.   O, I am slain!
[*Iago comes forward, wounds Cassio from behind, and
                                                   exits.*]
  Cas. I am maimed for ever. Help, ho! Murder! murder!   30
                              [*Falls.*]

Enter *Othello*.

  Oth. The voice of Cassio. Iago keeps his word.
  Rod. O, villain that I am!
  Oth.   It is even so.
  Cas. O, help, ho! light! a surgeon!
  Oth. 'Tis he. O brave Iago, honest and just,   35
That hast such noble sense of thy friend's wrong!
Thou teachest me. Minion, your dear lies dead,
And your unblest fate hies. Strumpet, I come.
Forth of my heart those charms, thine eyes, are blotted.
Thy bed, lust-stained, shall with lust's blood be spotted. 40
                              Exit.

41. **No passage:** no passers-by
47. **heavy:** heavily overcast
63. **spoiled:** mutilated

Enter Lodovico and Gratiano.

Cas. What, ho? No watch? No passage? Murder! murder!

Gra. 'Tis some mischance. The cry is very direful.

Cas. O, help!

Lod. Hark!   45

Rod. O wretched villain!

Lod. Two or three groan. It is a heavy night.
These may be counterfeits. Let's think't unsafe
To come in to the cry without more help.

Rod. Nobody come? Then shall I bleed to death.   50

Lod. Hark!

Enter Iago.

Gra. Here's one comes in his shirt, with light and weapons.

Iago. Who's there? Whose noise is this that cries on murder?   55

Lod. We do not know.

Iago.   Did not you hear a cry?

Cas. Here, here! For heaven's sake, help me!

Iago.   What's the matter?

Gra. This is Othello's ancient, as I take it.   60

Lod. The same indeed, a very valiant fellow.

Iago. What are you here that cry so grievously?

Cas. Iago? O, I am spoiled, undone by villains!
Give me some help.

Iago. O me, Lieutenant! What villains have done this?   65

Cas. I think that one of them is hereabout
And cannot make away.

Iago.   O treacherous villains!
What are you there? Come in, and give some help.
                [*To Lodovico and Gratiano.*]
Rod. O, help me here!   70
Cas. That's one of them.
Iago.   O murd'rous slave! O villain!
                [*Stabs Roderigo.*]
Rod. O damned Iago! O inhuman dog!
Iago. Kill men i' the dark? Where be these bloody
     thieves?   75
How silent is this town! Ho! murder! murder!
What may you be? Are you of good or evil?
Lod. As you shall prove us, praise us.
Iago. Signior Lodovico?
Lod. He, sir.   80
Iago. I cry you mercy. Here's Cassio hurt by villains.
Gra. Cassio?
Iago. How is it, brother?
Cas. My leg is cut in two.
Iago.   Marry, heaven forbid!   85
Light, gentlemen. I'll bind it with my shirt.

Enter *Bianca.*

Bian. What is the matter, ho? Who is't that cried?
Iago. Who is't that cried?
Bian. O my dear Cassio! my sweet Cassio!
O Cassio, Cassio, Cassio!   90
Iago. O notable strumpet!—Cassio, may you suspect
Who they should be that thus have mangled you?
Cas. No.

96. **chair:** litter

108. **cry you gentle pardon:** beg that you will be kind enough to pardon me

119. **Save you your labor:** don't bother (to minister to Cassio).

Gra. I am sorry to find you thus. I have been to seek
   you.   95
Iago. Lend me a garter. So. O for a chair
To bear him easily hence!
   Bian. Alas, he faints! O Cassio, Cassio, Cassio!
   Iago. Gentlemen all, I do suspect this trash
To be a party in this injury.—   100
Patience awhile, good Cassio.—Come, come!
Lend me a light. Know we this face or no?
Alas, my friend and my dear countryman
Roderigo? No. Yes, sure. O heaven! Roderigo.
   Gra. What, of Venice?   105
   Iago. Even he, sir. Did you know him?
   Gra.   Know him? Ay.
   Iago. Signior Gratiano? I cry you gentle pardon.
These bloody accidents must excuse my manners
That so neglected you.   110
   Gra.   I am glad to see you.
   Iago. How do you, Cassio?—O, a chair, a chair!
   Gra. Roderigo?
   Iago. He, he, 'tis he! [*A chair brought in*] O, that's
   well said! the chair.   115
Some good man bear him carefully from hence.
I'll fetch the General's surgeon. [*To Bianca*] For you,
   mistress,
Save you your labor.—He that lies slain here, Cassio,
Was my dear friend. What malice was between you?   120
   Cas. None in the world; nor do I know the man.
   Iago. [*To Bianca*] What, look you pale?—O, bear him
   out o' th' air.
                    [*Cassio and Roderigo are borne off.*]

125. **gastness:** terror
147. **tell's:** tell us
151. **fordoes:** destroys

Stay you, good gentlemen.—Look you pale, mistress?—
Do you perceive the gastness of her eye?—   125
Nay, an you stare, we shall hear more anon.
Behold her well; I pray you look upon her.
Do you see, gentlemen? Nay, guiltiness will speak,
Though tongues were out of use.

Enter *Emilia*.

   Emil. 'Las, what's the matter? What's the matter, hus- 130
     band?
   Iago. Cassio hath here been set on in the dark
By Roderigo, and fellows that are scaped.
He's almost slain, and Roderigo dead.
   Emil. Alas, good gentleman! alas, good Cassio!   135
   Iago. This is the fruit of whoring. Prithee, Emilia,
Go know of Cassio where he supped tonight.
[*To Bianca*] What, do you shake at that?
   Bian. He supped at my house; but I therefore shake
     not.   140
   Iago. O, did he so? I charge you go with me.
   Emil. Fie, fie upon thee, strumpet!
   Bian. I am no strumpet, but of life as honest
As you that thus abuse me.
   Emil.   As I? Foh! fie upon thee!   145
   Iago. Kind gentlemen, let's go see poor Cassio dressed.
[*To Bianca*] Come, mistress, you must tell's another tale.—
Emilia, run you to the citadel
And tell my lord and lady what hath happed.—
Will you go on afore? [*Aside*] This is the night   150
That either makes me or fordoes me quite.

Exeunt.

V. ii. The play moves rapidly to its climax in this final scene. Othello contemplates the sleeping Desdemona and is tempted by her beauty almost to disbelieve his suspicions. He hardens his heart, however, and when she awakes he accuses her once more of infidelity and finally smothers her. Emilia knocks at the door and is presently admitted. When she discovers that Desdemona is dead, she berates Othello for believing in Desdemona's guilt and calls for help against the murderer. When Iago and others come in response to her cries, Othello justifies his action as a defense of honor and discloses Iago's knowledge of the guilt of his wife with Cassio. Emilia reveals the villainy of her husband, and he stabs her fatally. Othello, now fully conscious of what he has done, tries to kill Iago but is restrained. He stabs himself and dies beside Desdemona. Iago is led away to torture and execution.

        ▪▪▪▪▪▪▪▪▪▪▪▪▪▪▪▪▪▪▪▪▪▪▪▪▪▪▪▪▪

5. **alablaster.** alabaster
8. **minister:** servant
13. **relume:** relight
21. **cruel:** that is, not provoked by mercy
21-2. **This sorrow's heavenly,/ It strikes where it doth love:** this sorrow is like that of God, who punishes the sinner while loving him.

Scene II. [Cyprus. A bedchamber in the Castle.]

Desdemona in her bed. Enter *Othello* with a light.

Oth. It is the cause, it is the cause, my soul.
Let me not name it to you, you chaste stars!
It is the cause. Yet I'll not shed her blood,
Nor scar that whiter skin of hers than snow,
And smooth as monumental alablaster.   5
Yet she must die, else she'll betray more men.
Put out the light, and then put out the light.
If I quench thee, thou flaming minister,
I can again thy former light restore,
Should I repent me; but once put out thy light,   10
Thou cunning'st pattern of excelling nature,
I know not where is that Promethean heat
That can thy light relume. When I have plucked the rose,
I cannot give it vital growth again;
It needs must wither. I'll smell it on the tree.   15
                                        He kisses her.
O balmy breath, that dost almost persuade
Justice to break her sword! One more, one more!
Be thus when thou art dead, and I will kill thee,
And love thee after. One more, and this the last!
So sweet was ne'er so fatal. I must weep,   20
But they are cruel tears. This sorrow's heavenly,
It strikes where it doth love. She wakes.
    Des. Who's there? Othello?
    Oth.   Ay, Desdemona.
    Des. Will you come to bed, my lord?   25
    Oth. Have you prayed tonight, Desdemon?

32. **walk by:** stand aside
34. **forfend:** forbid

Des.   Ay, my lord.

Oth. If you bethink yourself of any crime
Unreconciled as yet to heaven and grace,
Solicit for it straight.   30

Des. Alack, my lord, what may you mean by that?

Oth. Well, do it, and be brief; I will walk by.
I would not kill thy unprepared spirit.
No, heaven forfend! I would not kill thy soul.

Des. Talk you of killing?   35

Oth.   Ay, I do.

Des.   Then heaven
Have mercy on me!

Oth.   Amen, with all my heart!

Des. If you say so, I hope you will not kill me.   40

Oth. Humh!

Des. And yet I fear you; for you are fatal then
When your eyes roll so. Why I should fear I know not,
Since guiltiness I know not; but yet I feel I fear.

Oth. Think on thy sins.   45

Des.   They are loves I bear to you.

Oth. Ay, and for that thou diest.

Des. That death's unnatural that kills for loving.
Alas, why gnaw you so your nether lip?
Some bloody passion shakes your very frame.   50
These are portents; but yet I hope, I hope,
They do not point on me.

Oth.   Peace and be still!

Des. I will so. What's the matter?

Oth. That handkerchief which I so loved and gave thee 55
Thou gav'st to Cassio.

Des.   No, by my life and soul!
Send for the man and ask him.

74-6. **thou dost stone my heart,/ And mak'st me call what I intend to do/ A murder, which I thought a sacrifice:** that is, your stubborn refusal to show penitence, pray for your sins, and meekly submit is so arousing my passion that my killing of you will resemble murder instead of the sacrifice to divine justice I intended.

Oth.   Sweet soul, take heed,
Take heed of perjury; thou art on thy deathbed.   60
  Des. Ay, but not yet to die.
  Oth.   Yes, presently.
Therefore confess thee freely of thy sin;
For to deny each article with oath
Cannot remove nor choke the strong conception   65
That I do groan withal. Thou art to die.
  Des. Then Lord have mercy on me!
  Oth.   I say amen.
  Des. And have you mercy too! I never did
Offend you in my life; never loved Cassio   70
But with such general warranty of heaven
As I might love. I never gave him token.
  Oth. By heaven, I saw my handkerchief in's hand!
O perjured woman! thou dost stone my heart,
And mak'st me call what I intend to do   75
A murder, which I thought a sacrifice.
I saw the handkerchief.
  Des.   He found it then.
I never gave it him. Send for him hither.
Let him confess a truth.   80
  Oth.   He hath confessed.
  Des. What, my lord?
  Oth. That he hath used thee.
  Des.   How? unlawfully?
  Oth.   Ay.   85
  Des. He will not say so.
  Oth.   No, his mouth is stopped.
Honest Iago hath ta'en order for't.
  Des. O, my fear interprets. What, is he dead?

91. **stomach**: appetite

99. **Being done, there is no pause:** since this is the end, delay is impossible.

Oth. Had all his hairs been lives, my great revenge   90
Had stomach for them all.

Des. Alas, he is betrayed, and I undone!

Oth. Out, strumpet! Weep'st thou for him to my face?

Des. O, banish me, my lord, but kill me not!

Oth. Down, strumpet!   95

Des. Kill me tomorrow; let me live tonight!

Oth. Nay, an you strive—

Des. But half an hour!

Oth.   Being done, there is no pause.

Des. But while I say one prayer!   100

Oth.   It is too late.   *He smothers her.*
                              Emilia calls within, at the door.

Emil. My lord, my lord! What, ho, my lord, my lord!

Oth. What noise is this? Not dead? not yet quite dead?
I that am cruel am yet merciful;
I would not have thee linger in thy pain.   105
So, so.

Emil. [*Within*] What, ho! my lord, my lord!

Oth.   Who's there?

Emil. [*Within*] O, good my lord, I would speak a word
    with you!   110

Oth. Yes.—'Tis Emilia.—By-and-by.—She's dead.—
'Tis like she comes to speak of Cassio's death:
The noise was high. Ha! no more moving?
Still as the grave.—Shall she come in? Were't good?—
I think she stirs again. No.—What's best to do?   115
If she come in, she'll sure speak to my wife.
My wife! my wife! what wife? I have no wife.
O, insupportable! O heavy hour!
Methinks it should be now a huge eclipse

121. **yawn at alteration:** gape in an earthquake as an indication of the unsettled cosmic order

131. **error:** aberration, wandering from her usual course

Of sun and moon, and that th' affrighted globe   120
Should yawn at alteration.
    Emil.   [*Within*] I do beseech you
That I may speak with you, O good my lord!
    Oth. I had forgot thee. O, come in, Emilia.
Soft, by-and-by.—Let me the curtains draw.—   125
Where art thou?   [*Opens the door.*]

Enter *Emilia.*

           What's the matter with thee now?
    Emil. O my good lord, yonder's foul murder done!
    Oth. What? Now?
    Emil. But now, my lord.   130
    Oth. It is the very error of the moon.
She comes more near the earth than she was wont
And makes men mad.
    Emil. Cassio, my lord, hath killed a young Venetian
Called Roderigo.   135
    Oth.   Roderigo killed?
And Cassio killed?
    Emil.   No, Cassio is not killed.
    Oth. Not Cassio killed? Then murder's out of tune,
And sweet revenge grows harsh.   140
    Des. O, falsely, falsely murdered!
    Emil.   O Lord! what cry is that?
    Oth. That? What?
    Emil. Out and alas! that was my lady's voice.
Help! help, ho! help! O lady, speak again!   145
Sweet Desdemona! O sweet mistress, speak!
    Des. A guiltless death I die.
    Emil. O, who hath done this deed?

159. **folly:** unchastity
161. **false as water:** a proverbial idea because of the instability of water, which assumes the shape of any vessel into which it is put

Des. Nobody—I myself. Farewell.
Commend me to my kind lord. O, farewell!   *She dies.* 150
   Oth. Why, how should she be murd'red?
   Emil.   Alas, who knows?
   Oth. You heard her say herself, it was not I.
   Emil. She said so. I must needs report a truth.
   Oth. She's like a liar gone to burning hell!   155
'Twas I that killed her.
   Emil.   O, the more angel she,
And you the blacker devil!
   Oth. She turned to folly, and she was a whore.
   Emil. Thou dost belie her, and thou art a devil.   160
   Oth. She was false as water.
   Emil.   Thou art rash as fire to say
That she was false. O, she was heavenly true!
   Oth. Cassio did top her. Ask thy husband else.
O, I were damned beneath all depth in hell   165
But that I did proceed upon just grounds
To this extremity. Thy husband knew it all.
   Emil. My husband?
   Oth. Thy husband.
   Emil. That she was false to wedlock?   170
   Oth. Ay, with Cassio. Nay, had she been true,
If heaven would make me such another world
Of one entire and perfect chrysolite,
I'd not have sold her for it.
   Emil. My husband?   175
   Oth.   Ay, 'twas he that told me first.
An honest man he is, and hates the slime
That sticks on filthy deeds.
   Emil.   My husband?

180. **iterance:** repetition

182. **villainy hath made mocks with love:** a villain has used (your) love as a plaything.

194. **Peace, you were best:** you had better hold your peace.

195-96. **Thou hast not half the power to do me harm/ As I have to be hurt:** Emilia means that Othello can only destroy her physical being; he cannot affect her inner well-being.

Oth. What needs this iterance, woman? I say, thy 180
   husband.

Emil. O mistress, villainy hath made mocks with love!
My husband say that she was false?

Oth.   He, woman.
I say, thy husband. Dost understand the word?   185
My friend, thy husband; honest, honest Iago.

Emil. If he say so, may his pernicious soul
Rot half a grain a day! he lies to the heart.
She was too fond of her most filthy bargain.

Oth. Ha!   190

Emil. Do thy worst.
This deed of thine is no more worthy heaven
Than thou wast worthy her.

Oth.   Peace, you were best.

Emil. Thou hast not half the power to do me harm 195
As I have to be hurt. O gull! O dolt!
As ignorant as dirt! thou hast done a deed—
I care not for thy sword; I'll make thee known,
Though I lost twenty lives. Help! help, ho! help!
The Moor hath killed my mistress! Murder! murder!   200

   Enter *Montano, Gratiano, Iago,* and others.

Mon. What is the matter? How now, General?

Emil. O, are you come, Iago? You have done well,
That men must lay their murders on your neck.

Gra. What is the matter?

Emil. Disprove this villain, if thou be'st a man: 205
He says thou told'st him that his wife was false.
I know thou didst not; thou'rt not such a villain.
Speak, for my heart is full.

Iago. I told him what I thought, and told no more
Than what he found himself was apt and true.   210
   Emil. But did you ever tell him she was false?
   Iago. I did.
   Emil. You told a lie, an odious damned lie!
Upon my soul, a lie! a wicked lie!
She false with Cassio? Did you say with Cassio?   215
   Iago. With Cassio, mistress. Go to, charm your tongue.
   Emil. I will not charm my tongue; I am bound to
    speak:
My mistress here lies murdered in her bed—
   All. O heavens forfend!   220
   Emil. And your reports have set the murder on.
   Oth. Nay, stare not, masters. It is true indeed.
   Gra. 'Tis a strange truth.
   Mon. O monstrous act!
   Emil.   Villainy, villainy, villainy!   225
I think upon't, I think! I smell't! O villainy!
I thought so then. I'll kill myself for grief.
O villainy, villainy!
   Iago. What, are you mad? I charge you get you home.
   Emil. Good gentlemen, let me have leave to speak.   230
'Tis proper I obey him, but not now.
Perchance, Iago, I will ne'er go home.
   Oth. O! O! O!   *Falls on the bed.*
   Emil.   Nay, lay thee down and roar!
For thou hast killed the sweetest innocent   235
That e'er did lift up eye.
   Oth.   O, she was foul!   [*Rises.*]
I scarce did know you, uncle. There lies your niece,
Whose breath, indeed, these hands have newly stopped.
I know this act shows horrible and grim.   240

243. **Shore:** cut
244. **turn:** act
246. **reprobance:** reprobation; unregenerate damnation
251. **recognizance:** acknowledgment
258. **liberal:** freely; **the North:** i.e., North wind

Gra. Poor Desdemon! I am glad thy father's dead.
Thy match was mortal to him, and pure grief
Shore his old thread in twain. Did he live now,
This sight would make him do a desperate turn;
Yea, curse his better angel from his side,   245
And fall to reprobance.

Oth. 'Tis pitiful; but yet Iago knows
That she with Cassio hath the act of shame
A thousand times committed. Cassio confessed it;
And she did gratify his amorous works   250
With that recognizance and pledge of love
Which I first gave her; I saw it in his hand:
It was a handkerchief, an antique token
My father gave my mother.

Emil.   O God! O heavenly pow'rs!   255

Iago. Zounds, hold your peace!

Emil.   'Twill out, 'twill out! I peace?
No, I will speak as liberal as the North.
Let heaven and men and devils, let them all,
All, all, cry shame against me, yet I'll speak.   260

Iago. Be wise, and get you home.

Emil.   I will not.

              [*Iago draws and threatens Emilia.*]

Gra.   Fie!
Your sword upon a woman?

Emil. O thou dull Moor, that handkerchief thou   265
     speak'st of
I found by fortune, and did give my husband;
For often with a solemn earnestness
(More than indeed belonged to such a trifle)
He begged of me to steal't.   270

Iago.   Villainous whore!

276. **coxcomb**: fool, the term often applied to the professional jester whose cap simulated a cock's comb

278. **stones**: lightning bolts

283. **notorious**: remarkable

288. **I am not valiant neither**: that is, my courage is gone as well as my good conscience.

289. **whipster**: contemptible fellow

290. **why should honor outlive honesty**: why should the reputation outlive the reality of honor.

Emil. She give it Cassio? No, alas, I found it,
And I did give't my husband.
   Iago.   Filth, thou liest!
   Emil. By heaven, I do not, I do not, gentlemen.   275
O murd'rous coxcomb! what should such a fool
Do with so good a wife?
   Oth.   Are there no stones in heaven
But what serves for the thunder? Precious villain!
   The Moor runs at Iago, [but is disarmed by Montano].
                        Iago kills his wife.
   Gra. The woman falls. Sure he hath killed his wife. 280
   Emil. Ay, ay. O, lay me by my mistress' side.
                              Exit Iago.
   Gra. He's gone, but his wife's killed.
   Mon. 'Tis a notorious villain. Take you this weapon,
Which I have here recovered from the Moor.
Come, guard the door without. Let him not pass,   285
But kill him rather. I'll after that same villain,
For 'tis a damned slave.
       Exeunt Montano and Gratiano [with others.
            Manent Othello and Emilia].
   Oth.   I am not valiant neither;
But every puny whipster gets my sword.
But why should honor outlive honesty?   290
Let it go all.
   Emil.   What did thy song bode, lady?
Hark, canst thou hear me? I will play the swan,
And die in music. [*Sings*] "Willow, willow, willow."
Moor, she was chaste; she loved thee, cruel Moor.   295
So come my soul to bliss as I speak true.
So speaking as I think, I die, I die.   *She dies.*

299. **the ice-brook's temper:** tempered in ice-cold water, as were some Spanish blades

304. **naked:** unarmed

311. **your stop:** your ability to hinder

314. **butt:** structure holding the target in archery; thus, the limit of the arrow's flight

315. **seamark:** identifying landmark of a ship's destination

316. **lost:** vain

317. **a rush:** a bulrush; an insignificant weapon

320. **at compt:** on the day of judgment

321. **This look of thine:** the innocence on your face (which will prove his deed a murder, not an act of justice)

Oth. I have another weapon in this chamber;
It is a sword of Spain, the ice-brook's temper.
O, here it is.—Uncle, I must come forth.   300
   Gra. (Within) If thou attempt it, it will cost thee dear.
Thou hast no weapon, and perforce must suffer.
   Oth. Look in upon me then and speak with me,
Or, naked as I am, I will assault thee.

[Enter *Gratiano*.]

   Gra. What is the matter?   305
   Oth.   Behold, I have a weapon.
A better never did itself sustain
Upon a soldier's thigh. I have seen the day
That with this little arm and this good sword
I have made my way through more impediments   310
Than twenty times your stop. But O vain boast!
Who can control his fate? 'Tis not so now.
Be not afraid, though you do see me weaponed.
Here is my journey's end, here is my butt,
And very seamark of my utmost sail.   315
Do you go back dismayed? 'Tis a lost fear.
Man but a rush against Othello's breast,
And he retires. Where should Othello go?—
Now, how dost thou look now? O ill-starred wench!
Pale as thy smock! When we shall meet at compt,   320
This look of thine will hurl my soul from heaven,
And fiends will snatch at it. Cold, cold, my girl?
Even like thy chastity.—O cursed slave!
Whip me, ye devils,
From the possession of this heavenly sight!   325
Blow me about in winds! roast me in sulphur!

333. **I look down towards his feet:** that is, look to see whether he has cloven feet like Satan

Wash me in steep-down gulfs of liquid fire!
O Desdemona, Desdemona! dead!
O! O! O!

Enter *Lodovico, Cassio, Montano,* and *Iago,*
with *Officers.*

Lod. Where is this rash and most unfortunate man? 330
Oth. That's he that was Othello. Here I am.
Lod. Where is that viper? Bring the villain forth.
Oth. I look down towards his feet—but that's a fable.
If that thou be'st a devil, I cannot kill thee.

[*Wounds Iago.*]

Lod. Wrench his sword from him. 335

[*Othello is disarmed.*]

Iago. I bleed, sir, but not killed.
Oth. I am not sorry neither. I'd have thee live;
For in my sense, 'tis happiness to die.
Lod. O thou Othello that wert once so good,
Fall'n in the practice of a damned slave, 340
What shall be said to thee?
Oth. Why, anything:
An honorable murderer, if you will;
For naught did I in hate, but all in honor.
Lod. This wretch hath part confessed his villainy. 345
Did you and he consent in Cassio's death?
Oth. Ay.
Cas. Dear General, I never gave you cause.
Oth. I do believe it, and I ask your pardon.
Will you, I pray, demand that demi-devil 350
Why he hath thus ensnared my soul and body?

356. **thou dost best:** Iago is correct to be silent since his crimes are too horrible to be spoken of
364. **gross:** flagrant
368. **belike:** doubtless
380. **Brave me:** provoke me to a quarrel
381. **cast:** dismissed; see II. [iii.] 15.

Iago. Demand me nothing. What you know, you know.
From this time forth I never will speak word.
  Lod. What, not to pray?
  Gra.   Torments will ope your lips. 355
  Oth. Well, thou dost best.
  Lod. Sir, you shall understand what hath befall'n,
Which, as I think, you know not. Here is a letter
Found in the pocket of the slain Roderigo;
And here another. The one of them imports   360
The death of Cassio to be undertook
By Roderigo.
  Oth. O villain!
  Cas.   Most heathenish and most gross!
  Lod. Now here's another discontented paper   365
Found in his pocket too; and this, it seems,
Roderigo meant t' have sent this damned villain;
But that, belike, Iago in the interim
Came in and satisfied him.
  Oth.   O thou pernicious caitiff!— 370
How came you, Cassio, by that handkerchief
That was my wife's?
  Cas.   I found it in my chamber;
And he himself confessed but even now
That there he dropped it for a special purpose   375
Which wrought to his desire.
  Oth.   O fool! fool! fool!
  Cas. There is besides in Roderigo's letter,
How he upbraids Iago that he made him
Brave me upon the watch; whereon it came   380
That I was cast; and even but now he spake,
After long seeming dead—Iago hurt him,
Iago set him on.

389. **close prisoner rest**: remain a closely guarded prisoner

390. **Till that**: until

392. **Soft you**: hold.

399. **wrought**: worked upon

400. **Perplexed**: distracted by doubts

401. **the base Indian**: an ignorant Indian unaware of the value of a precious stone

411. **period**: ending

Lod. You must forsake this room and go with us.
Your power and your command is taken off,   385
And Cassio rules in Cyprus. For this slave,
If there be any cunning cruelty
That can torment him much and hold him long,
It shall be his. You shall close prisoner rest
Till that the nature of your fault be known   390
To the Venetian state. Come, bring away.
 Oth. Soft you! a word or two before you go.
I have done the state some service, and they know't—
No more of that. I pray you, in your letters,
When you shall these unlucky deeds relate,   395
Speak of me as I am. Nothing extenuate,
Nor set down aught in malice. Then must you speak
Of one that loved not wisely, but too well;
Of one not easily jealous, but, being wrought,
Perplexed in the extreme; of one whose hand   400
(Like the base Indian) threw a pearl away
Richer than all his tribe; of one whose subdued eyes,
Albeit unused to the melting mood,
Drop tears as fast as the Arabian trees
Their med'cinable gum. Set you down this;   405
And say besides that in Aleppo once,
Where a malignant and a turbaned Turk
Beat a Venetian and traduced the state,
I took by the throat the circumcised dog
And smote him—thus.   *He stabs himself.* 410
 Lod. O bloody period!
 Gra.   All that's spoke is marred.
 Oth. I kissed thee ere I killed thee. No way but this—
Killing myself, to die upon a kiss.
                    He [falls across Desdemona and] dies.

417. **Spartan dog**: the dogs of Sparta were renowned for their fierceness as the men of Sparta were known for their stoicism.

418. **fell**: fierce

421. **keep**: guard

Cas. This did I fear, but thought he had no weapon; 415
For he was great of heart.

Lod.   O Spartan dog,
More fell than anguish, hunger, or the sea!
Look on the tragic loading of this bed.
This is thy work. The object poisons sight;   420
Let it be hid. Gratiano, keep the house,
And seize upon the fortunes of the Moor,
For they succeed on you. To you, Lord Governor,
Remains the censure of this hellish villain.
The time, the place, the torture—O, enforce it!   425
Myself will straight aboard, and to the state
This heavy act with heavy heart relate.

Exeunt omnes.

A fellow almost damned in a fair wife [Iago—I. i. 22]

. . . I will wear my heart upon my sleeve [Iago—I. i. 68]

. . . one of those that will not serve God if the devil bid you [Iago—I. i. 121–122]

She swore . . . 'twas strange, 'twas passing strange [Othello—I. iii. 176]

. . . as tenderly be led by the nose As asses are [Iago—I. iii. 419–420]

I am nothing if not critical [Iago—II. i. 137]

To suckle fools and chronicle small beer [Iago—II. i. 189]

When devils will the blackest sins put on, They do suggest at first with heavenly shows [Iago—II. iii. 353–354]

Good name in man and woman, dear my lord, Is the immediate jewel of their souls. [Iago—III. iii. 180–181]

O, beware, my lord, of jealousy! It is the green-eyed monster [Iago—III. iii. 191–192]

Trifles light as air Are to the jealous confirmations strong

As proofs of holy writ. [Iago—III. iii. 364–366]

Not poppy nor mandragora, Nor all the drowsy syrups of the world, Shall ever medicine thee to that sweet sleep Which thou ow'dst yesterday. [Iago—III. iii. 373–376]

O, now, for ever Farewell the tranquil mind . . . Othello's occupation's gone! [Othello—III. iii. 392–402]

Heaven truly knows that thou art false as hell. [Othello—IV. ii. 48]

It is the cause, it is the cause, my soul. [Othello—V. ii. 1]

She was false as water. [Othello—V. ii. 161]

As ignorant as dirt! [Emilia—V. ii. 197]

Here is my journey's end, here is my butt, And very seamark of my utmost sail. [Othello—V. ii. 314–315]

. . . one that loved not wisely, but too well [Othello—V. ii. 396-398]